"**Catholic literature,** doctrinal and devotional, owes a great deal to Mother Mary Loyola. There is a certain wholesomeness, naturalness, geniality about her spirituality that at once wins a place in the Catholic heart for whatever she writes." --The Ecclesiastical Review, volume 58, January 1918

About Mother Mary Loyola:
    Most Catholics today who have heard the name Mother Mary Loyola know her as the author of *The King of the Golden City*, which has enjoyed a resurgence in popularity in recent years. But few know that she wrote over two dozen works, and that she was once a household name among Catholics of her era. What made her unique among Catholic authors was her ability to draw in her listeners with story after story—and not just any stories, but ones that incorporated current events and brand new inventions of the time. Despite the fact that those events are no longer current, and those inventions no longer brand new, her books scintillate with the appeal of an active mind that could find a moral in the most unusual places. And while the printed word lacks the animated facial expressions and vocal inflections which reveal a gifted storyteller, hers convey her enthusiasm so capably that the reader can easily imagine sitting at the feet of this wise old nun.

About *Coram Sanctissimo*:
    "Mother Mary Loyola needs no introduction to attract us to a new book from her pen, but it is a distinct addition to it to have Father Thurston's historical outline of the growth of the devotion to the Blessed Sacrament. As the name indicates, this little book is intended for those visiting the Blessed Sacrament. The aids are mostly not prayers, but thoughts calculated to set the stream of prayerful affections flowing, and the authoress knows how to select the kind of thoughts which will appeal to our modern and theorizing hearts. Interspersed with the prose are some verses which, as the Preface tells us, she hesitated to insert. The reader will be glad she overcame her reluctance."
— *The Month*, April 1901.

To learn more about Mother Mary Loyola, visit our website at
www.staugustineacademypress.com.

## VISITE AU St SACREMENT.

Parlez Seigneur, votre servante écoute;
ouvrez son oreille secrète et dites à mon âme:
JE SUIS LA SOURCE DE TON SALUT.

# Coram Sanctissimo
## Before the Most Holy

BY

## Mother Mary Loyola
### of the Bar Convent, York

Edited by

Rev. Herbert Thurston, S.J.

2012
St. Augustine Academy Press
Lisle, Illinois

This book is newly typeset based on the twelfth edition published in 1909 by B. Herder. All editing strictly limited to the correction of errors in the original text and minor clarifications in punctuation or phrasing. Any remaining oddities of spelling or phrasing are as found in the original.

*Nihil Obstat*
HERBERT THURSTON, S.J.
*Censor Deputatus*

*Imprimatur*
HERBERTUS CARD. VAUGHAN
*Archiep. Westmonast.*

5th September, 1900.

This book was originally published in 1902 by Sands & Co. This edition ©2012 by St. Augustine Academy Press. All editing by Lisa Bergman.

ISBN: 978-1-936639-20-5
Library of Congress Control Number: 2012949169

Unless otherwise noted, all illustrations in this book, including the cover, are either the original illustrations as found in the book, or are public domain images.

*Frontispiece Illustration:*
Holy Card Heaven. http://holycardheaven.blogspot.com, October 22, 2010.

TO

JESUS CHRIST

YESTERDAY

TO-DAY

AND THE SAME

FOR EVER

# Contents

|  | Preface | ix |
|---|---|---|
| I | Visits | 1 |
| II | Praise | 6 |
| III | "Possumus." | 9 |
| IV | The Son of Man | 12 |
| V | What Things? | 14 |
| VI | Venite ad Me Omnes | 19 |
| VII | The Hidden God | 21 |
| VIII | Looking Through the Lattices | 23 |
| IX | Lord, Come and See! | 26 |
| X | Neglect | 28 |
| XI | Faith | 30 |
| XII | After a Defeat | 33 |
| XIII | After a Victory | 35 |
| XIV | A Divine Friend | 36 |
| XV | An Evening Visit | 38 |
| XVI | Privileged | 40 |
| XVII | The Improvidence of Love | 43 |
| XVIII | Changes | 45 |
| XIX | I Have Somewhat to Say to Thee | 47 |
| XX | A Divine Plaint | 50 |
| XXI | Thanksgiving | 52 |
| XXII | Darkness | 55 |
| XXIII | "What is Truth?" | 59 |
| XXIV | His Second Coming | 61 |

| | | |
|---:|:---|---:|
| XXV | Our Earth | 63 |
| XXVI | Christ Our Study | 66 |
| XXVII | Our Father | 69 |
| XXVIII | Hereafter | 70 |
| XXIX | My Vineyard | 72 |
| XXX | Where We Are True | 74 |
| XXXI | In Silence and in Hope | 76 |
| XXXII | God's Work | 78 |
| XXXIII | A Strong Cry | 81 |
| XXXIV | "Be Ready!" | 83 |
| XXXV | "Domine, Ecce quem Amas Infirmatur." | 85 |
| XXXVI | After a Death | 88 |
| XXXVII | God's Ways | 90 |
| XXXVIII | Twilight and Noon | 94 |
| XXXIV | Responsibility | 98 |
| XL | Life | 102 |

# *Preface*

THE custom of honouring the Eucharistic presence of Christ our Lord by paying "Visits" to the Blessed Sacrament may be quoted as one of the most conspicuous examples of development in the devotional practice of the Catholic Church. Down to the latter part of the Middle Ages such an usage seems to have been entirely unknown. As far as regards England, the late Father Bridgett, if I mistake not, says that in all the researches made by him while compiling his *History of the Holy Eucharist in Great Britain* he had not come across one clear example of a visit to the Blessed Sacrament in pre-Reformation times. Even on the Continent the idea of any extra-liturgical *cultus* of the Blessed Eucharist seems to have grown up very tardily. There were many saints as late as the fifteenth century—say, for example, St. Frances of Rome, whose lives show no trace of such a conception, though nothing could be more strongly emphasised than their devotion to the Blessed Sacrament in Holy Communion.[1] It is remarkable to notice that even St. Ignatius Loyola, in the book of the *Spiritual*

---

1 The earliest satisfactory example of visits to the Blessed Sacrament which I have so far come across occurs in the life of Blessed Maria de Malliaco (a.d. 1331-1414), who, it is stated, *"in festis solemnibus vigilabat in ecclesia coram corpore Christi."* The story of St. Louis of France, who in a grievous storm placed himself on his knees before the Blessed Sacrament on ship-board, does not appear to me to belong to quite the same category. I should be grateful to any readers of this note who may be able to supply me with earlier instances.

*Exercises*, when directing attention to the abiding presence of God with His creatures as a motive for awakening love, says not a word of the Blessed Sacrament. One must not, of course, press the negative argument too far. No prudent man would infer in this latter case that the practice of visiting churches to commune with our Lord in the Tabernacle was unknown in the sixteenth century, but it is reasonable to conclude that the uninterrupted Eucharistic presence of God with His people did not then play the same conspicuous part in the devotional life of the faithful that it does in our day.

This late and gradual development of a devotion, which seems to us now so natural and so unmistakably involved in premises that all men accepted, is certainly a remarkable fact. Even to the present day the Greek Church, though its belief in transubstantiation is no less explicit than our own, has never drawn the inference that out Lord has come in the Blessed Sacrament to be our companion and refuge as well as our food. It seems to have been part of the Divine dispensation, in this as in some other matters, to hold men's eyes that they should not know Him. Throughout the long centuries our forefathers seem to have regarded the Eucharistic presence as if Christ had wished to preserve His *incognito* while He dwelt amongst them, or as if He were sleeping as of old in the bark of Peter and would rebuke the want of faith of those who too importunately disturbed His repose. But surely we are right in thinking that if they so apprehended God's purpose in remaining on our altars, their appreciation of His boon was but inchoative and imperfect. To us now it seems so obvious that the work of Jesus Christ in the Blessed Sacrament was not meant to be intermittent, limited to the time of Mass and Holy Communion, that it is hard to believe that Christians who truly recognised this presence in their midst can ever have conceived otherwise. Perhaps we may draw the lesson that if the fulness of understanding were long delayed in so plain a matter, it is not surprising that in other dogmas and practices which justify themselves less obviously, there may be developments in the Church's teaching not suspected or at least not clearly apprehended by our forefathers in the faith.

As things are, no devout Catholic would wish to be deprived of the privilege of drawing near to our Saviour in the Tabernacle and making Him the daily confidant of hopes and fears, of joys and troubles. But what distresses many pious souls is that having Him ready and willing to listen they should so often find themselves tongue-tied in His presence. The set forms of prayer which they know by heart are worn threadbare by routine, and books too often prove stiff and artificial. The heart has many wants and longings, but hardly knows how to put them into words. In such a case real help, I think, is likely to be found in this very miscellaneous collection of musings, self-arraignments, out-pourings of spirit, to which the authoress has given the apt name of *Coram Sanctissimo*, "in the presence of the Most Holy." They are not intended to be taken in rotation, or to be used every day, but there are times when a troubled worshipper, turning over the leaves, may light upon something here which will chime in with his mood and will make the task of prayer more easy to him. And if for one or another the thoughts of this little book may serve to break the ice and to render the soul for the nonce more at home in that holy presence, I feel sure that the authoress will consider the labour spent in writing it to have been abundantly repaid.

It will be noticed that in the pages which follow verse finds a place as well as prose. It would not be fair to let this go forth to the world without stating that it has been written, so to speak, under protest, and that without strong encouragement Mother Mary Loyola would hardly have suffered it to see the light. Although the verses are perhaps unequal, I do not in any way repent the share I have had in urging the writer to let them stand. It would have been worth a greater risk of failure and a longer expenditure of time to have secured even a few such happy lines as may be read for instance in the chapter headed "In Silence and in Hope," describing St. Mary Magdalen:—

> She came with her crushing memories,
> She came with her secret fears,
> She brought Him her hidden misery
> And her bitter, burning tears.

Or again:—

> Absorbed in her loving ministries
> She knelt at His feet apart,
> The scandal of every eye save one
> That soundeth the secret heart.

The verses at best are only an experiment. They were written in each case for the sake of the thought, not of the metrical form, and if the authoress could have found, as she long endeavoured to do, any suitable religious poetry which expressed kindred ideas, and which would have afforded that variety which is meant to be characteristic of this little booklet, she would have been glad, I know, to escape the seeming presumption of appearing as a writer of verse. But I do not think that the many friends who use and appreciate Mother Loyola's *Confession and Communion* and her other devotional books will be disappointed in anything which may meet their eye in this new effort of her pen.

HERBERT THURSTON, S.J.
11TH SEPTEMBER, 1900

# I
# *Visits*

*Go to Him early in the morning, and let thy foot wear the steps of His doors.*
(Ecclus. vi. 36.)

How careful we are to observe the courtesies of life! How uneasy till such social duties are discharged! In the making and returning of calls, how fidgety if hindered, how sensible that delay demands apology!

And this where mere acquaintances are concerned. But what when there is question of a friend, a benefactor, one devoted to us and to our interests? If formal visits are here uncalled for, it is only because our heart needs no prompting. Uninvited, inconsiderately often, we come and go, "wearing the steps of his doors."

And our best of friends—do we treat Him thus?—as affectionately, as familiarly? If not, why not? Is He not among the benefactors whose gifts deserve thanks, the friends whose feelings have to be considered, the acquaintances, at least, whose attentions must be acknowledged? Is it because He puts Himself so completely at our disposal that He is to be neglected? Or because He is King of kings that He is to be considered outside the circle where courtesy is exacted?

Ah, Lord, how unmindful we are of what is due to You! How unmindful I am of Your unfailing devotedness to me! Sent into this world as into a strange neighbourhood, I found

You waiting to receive me, to make me welcome, to offer Your services, to show me all manner of graceful kindness. You have thrown open Your house to me. You invite me to Your table. You press upon me Your gifts: *"All ye that thirst, come to the waters...Come, buy wine and milk without money and without any price."*[1] *"Come to Me and I will refresh you."*[2] *"Him that cometh to Me, I will not cast out"*[3] You make use of every motive to draw me to Yourself; yet have to complain after all: *"You will not come to Me that you may have life."*[4]

"They began all at once to make excuse. I have bought a farm...I pray thee, hold me excused. I have bought five yoke of oxen...I pray thee, hold me excused. I have married a wife, and therefore I cannot come."[5]

Thus it was long ago; thus it is now. We have time for other duties—for our correspondence, our shopping, our afternoon calls on other more favoured friends. But no time for a visit to Him. Is it so far then to the nearest church? So far that He may well accept the distance as sufficient reason for our absence, except at times when attendance is of obligation? Can I urge home duties and necessary occupations, when I see who those are that can and do find time to visit Him?

O my Lord, why these wretched subterfuges with You, "the God of truth"?[6] Why not fall at Your feet and own that it is not distance, nor lack of leisure, nor any reasonable plea that keeps me from You, but simply and solely *the want of love?* It is a reason I could not give to any other friend. I should have to find some other pretext with which to colour my neglect. But with You there need be no dissembling. Your friendship stands alone in the perfect frankness and confidence permissible on both sides. We may own to being cold and half-unwilling visitors, yet we are not, for that, unwelcome. The petulance,

---

1 Isa. lv.     2 Matt. xi.     3 John vi.
4 *Ibid.* v.     5 Luke xiv.     6 Psa. xxx.

the selfishness, the waywardness of our moods that in the very interest of other friendships call for self-restraint, may show themselves in all their ugliness before the All-pitying, the Friend "more friendly than a brother,"[1] whom nothing can shock, disgust, estrange.

He wants our intercourse with Him to be perfectly free; nothing studied, nothing strained. He desires to have us as we are, no less than as we would be. He wants to be taken into our confidence, to be let into the secret chambers of our souls, into which we only peep ourselves at stated times and with half-averted glance. He would share in the interests and troubles of the moment; be called upon for sympathy in every event, great or small, that interrupts the even flow of our home life or of our inner life; take part in every experience, whether of sorrow or of joy. The soldier off to the front, the baby with its broken toy, the girl with her first secret, no less than the wife, the mother, the priest, with their burdened hearts— He wants them all. He sees us going off here and there for help, and comfort, and counsel. He hears our feet as they hurry past His door to wear the doorsteps of other friends, and He calls to us in those tones divine in their tenderness of reproach: "*You will not come to Me. My people have forsaken Me, the Fountain of living water, and have digged to themselves cisterns, broken cisterns, that can hold no water.*"[2]

How long, O Lord, how long? When shall we wake up to the reality of Your Presence in our midst, and to the purpose of that Presence? We would die for it if need be, and yet we heed it not. Shall I wait till it is brought home to me by the remorse of my last hour, or by the long, long hours of purgatory? Oh, why did I not make use of my Emmanuel, my God with me, whilst I had time, "whilst He was in the way with me"?[3] Why

---
1  Prov. xviii.          2  Jer. ii.          3  Matt. v.

during my dream-life down there did I not realise the need of Him that is the one need in this real life of eternity?

A child at catechism said: "Won't it be dreadful for those who don't believe in the Real Presence to find at Judgment that it *was* real, that our Lord was there after all! Even if they didn't know any better, and so it was not their fault, and our Lord is not angry with them—I think they will be so dreadfully sorry all the same."

But if these will be sorry, what will be the case of those who did know, and neglected Him? Those to whom He will say, "*So long a time have I been with you, and you have not known Me!*"[1] "*I was daily with you in the temple.*"[2]

Lord Jesus, let not that be my bitterest thought in purgatory, that land of bitter thoughts. It is time that Your love should be returned, that I should make amends for the past, that I should hasten to You with my sorrow and my love.

*Go to Him early in the morning.* Is daily Mass an impossibility in my case? He waits for me there, to offer, for me and with me, His sacrifice and mine for the interests we share together.

*And let thy feet wear the steps of His doors.* More especially in the afternoon or evening, when the church is quiet and He is left all alone. With a little goodwill and ingenuity could I not include a visit to Him in my weekly, if not in my daily programme? Could I not so arrange my calls to other friends as to leave a few moments for my dearest and my best? How blessed a remembrance, when He is brought to my doors at the last, to be my viaticum, that in life I was faithful to the duties of friendship and wore the steps of His doors!

---

1   John xiv.          2   Luke xxii.

# Visits

O blessed, self-sufficing God
  Athirst for me,
Coming a beggar to my door
  All suppliantly,
Craving with meek persistence alms
  Of my poor heart,
A thought, a word of sympathy—how sweet,
  How sweet Thou art!

And must Thou knock and ever knock
  Till life is flown,
Seeking vain entrance to a heart
  That is Thine own?
Or wilt Thou rather work this hour
  Such change in me
That hither I may come "wearing Thy steps"
  Athirst for Thee!

## II
## *Praise*

*Give praise to our God, all ye His servants,*
*and you that fear Him, little and great.*
(Apoc. xix. 5.)

WHEN heaven is opened for an instant it is to let out a burst of praise. "*Glory to God in the highest!*"[1] "*Thou art worthy, O Lord our God, to receive glory, and honour, and power!*"[2] "*The Lamb that was slain, is worthy to receive power, and divinity, and wisdom, and strength, and honour, and glory, and benediction...To Him that sitteth on the throne, and to the Lamb, benediction and honour and glory and power for ever and ever.*"[3]

We lift up our heads; we are rapt. It is an unexpected strain from fatherland that catches the exile's ear and thrills through every fibre of his being. It finds an affinity, that burst of praise, in every human soul on which the sense of exile weighs. For it is the strain to which every soul is attuned by the very fact of its creation. The language of praise is our mother-tongue. *Gementes et flentes in hac lacrymarum valle* was no part of God's original design for us. We took the golden harps out of His hand and strained and broke the strings, and now the notes are plaintive when not discordant. But Christ has restored all things. He has brought back our joy by taking our sorrow on

---

1  Luke ii.      2  Apoc. iv.      3  *Ibid.* v.

Himself. Because here on earth He prayed "with a strong cry and tears"[1] the song of praise is to be put again upon our lips. Yet a little while and "God shall wipe away all tears...and death shall be no more, nor mourning, nor crying, nor sorrow shall be any more."[2] He is here upon the altar, waiting to catch up the faint accents of my praise, and bear them with His own before the throne of God.

Do this for me, O dearest Lord. Praise does not come easily to these lips of mine. The cares of life, and its failures, and its pains; heaviness of soul, and the weight of the corruptible body, with all the engrossingness of self, wring my heart dry of praise. A sudden revelation of Your goodness in the removal of a trial, or the advent of an unlooked-for joy, will lighten it for a moment and lift it up to You in benediction. Yet even this impulse of thankful love is weak and cannot long sustain itself, and I fall again humbled at Your feet, to feel how little I can do and say even at my best. As to the pure praise of heaven—free of all thought of self, where self is drowned in the glad, triumphant, all-absorbing sense of Your greatness, and grandeur, and all-sufficingness—of this I know nothing. Yet it is the language of my country, the tongue I shall speak for ever—should I not be learning it here in time? A language may be learned in a foreign land though the accent we only catch on its own soil.

Often and often, dear Master, I say to You with the Twelve, "Teach me to pray." I say to You now, "Teach me to praise." Teach me that highest, purest prayer which will be the incense rising for ever from my heart when other prayer has ceased.

Fuller and richer every hour grows the heavenly harmony, as part after part is taken up by the blessed choristers arriving from earth and purgatory. But for whom are reserved the

---

1  Heb. v.    2  Apoc. xxi.

richest notes in the anthem, entoned with human voice by Christ Himself? Surely for those who have practised that praise even here *in hac lacrymarum valle*. Whose hearts have never been allowed, even in exile, to forget the tongue of fatherland. Which have leaped up day by day in the *Gloria in excelsis* and the *Magnificat*, in the *Benedictus* and the *Te Deum*. Which have persisted in praise when the heart was weighted heaviest; when doubt, repining, rebellion even, sought to stifle its voice. They heard the call: "*Arise, give praise in the night.*"[1] And answered: "*The Lord gave, and the Lord hath taken away, as it hath pleased the Lord, so is it done: blessed be the name of the Lord.*"[2] It is this praise in the night that sounds sweetest in the ear of God. It is of these His faithful servants that He says: "*They shall praise Me in the land of their captivity, and shall be mindful of My name.*"[3]

What wonder that their song shall be sweetest in the City of Peace; that their voices shall mingle more intimately than the rest with hers whose heart was singing *Ecce ancilla*—even in its agony—with His Who, having sung a hymn, went forth to Calvary!

---

[1] Lament. ii.     [2] Job i.     [3] Baruch ii.

# III
# "*Possumus.*"

*"Can you drink of the chalice that I drink of?"*
*"We can."*
(Mark x. 38, 39.)

Far back in the ages before the world was, "*in the beginning*," I hear the Eternal Father treating with His co-equal Son about my redemption:

"Canst Thou for that soul and for its salvation go down from heaven and be made man?"

And the Divine Word answered: "*I can.*"

"Canst Thou live a life of thirty-three years, toiling and teaching and instituting Divine means for its salvation, and end that life of hardship and suffering by a death of pain and shame?"

"*I can.*"

"Canst Thou perpetuate that Incarnation and annihilation even to the end of time; hiding Thyself under the form of bread in order to meet it on its entrance into life, to be its companion, its refuge, its food all the days of its pilgrimage?"

"*I can.*"

"And when, O Lover of that soul, it shall meet Thy love, Thy advances, Thy sacrifices as Thou knowest it will meet them, canst Thou bear with it still, supporting its coldness, its waywardness, its indifference, its ingratitude?"

And Jesus said, "*I can.*"

And now my Redeemer turns to question me in my turn:

"Can you for the sake of your salvation co-operate with Me and turn to your own profit all I have done and am ready to do for you, resolving to avoid everything that would imperil the great work we have undertaken—all grievous sin and all venial sin that leads to mortal?"

What can I answer but, "O Lord, *I can*"—?

"Can you, as some return for My love, find it in your heart to avoid not only sin, but the infidelities which impede My work in your soul, obstruct My grace and hinder union between us?"

What is my answer now?

"Can you, with the eye of faith, see Me in My suffering members—the poor, the sick, the outcast, the unprotected, the little helpless children—and for My sake sacrifice leisure, or ease, or worldly means to succour and serve them?"

"Give me the faith, Lord, to recognise You in all these, and in the strength of that faith, *I can.*"

"Can you come after Me by taking up your cross daily—the cross I have laid upon you to liken you to Myself?"

"Yes, Lord, for beneath will be the everlasting arms. You will not leave me alone, and with Your help, *I can.*"

"Can you uphold My cause in the face of ridicule and disgrace—ready, if not glad, to suffer reproach for My name?"

"In Him Who strengtheneth me, Lord, *I can.*"

"Can you bear to be overlooked, set at naught, despised by the world as one at variance with its principles, as following another leader? Can you bear the taunt: '*And thou also wast with Jesus of Nazareth*' —?"

"Look on me, Lord, in hours of trial as You looked on Peter, and sustained by that glance, *I can*."

"Can you drink still deeper of My chalice—the chalice I drained for you—bearing with constancy desolation of spirit and the hiding of the Father's Face, content to serve Him for Himself rather than for His gifts?"

"In union, O my Lord, with Your desolate soul on Calvary, *I can*."

## IV
## *The Son of Man*

*"I also have a heart as well as you."*
(Job xii. 3.)

Our Lord does quite simply what some of us are too proud to do. He owns to the yearning felt by every human heart for the sympathy of its kind. He speaks plainly of His desire to share His joy and sorrows with His friends, and is at no pains to conceal His need of their support, His gratitude for their devotedness, His distress at their unfaithfulness and desertion. "Father, I will that where I am, they also whom Thou hast given Me may be with Me: that they may see My glory."[1] "You are they who have continued with Me in My temptations."[2] "My soul is sorrowful even unto death: stay you here, and watch with Me...Could you not watch one hour with Me?"[3] "The hour cometh...that you shall be scattered every man to his own, and shall leave Me alone."[4]

He comes to a weak woman for her compassion and her help. He asks her to spread abroad among His friends the words in which He unburdened His heart to her, and beg them to come and bear Him company in His life of solitude and neglect. To each one of us He says from the tabernacle: "Stay you here, and watch with Me...Could you not watch one hour with Me?" Or if not one hour, one quarter?

---

1  John xvii.　　　　2  Luke xxii.　　　　3  Matt. xxvi.
4  John xvi.

*Stay with Me* because I am going to offer My morning sacrifice, and men are too busy to assist at the oblation of Myself for them.

*Stay with Me* for a few moments at midday, when the glare of the world and its rush and its din are fiercest. Turn off the crowded pavement into the quiet church, "Come apart...and rest a little."[1]

*Stay with Me* because it is towards evening and the day is now far spent. There will be no more visitors for Me today, none through the long hours of the night. Stay with Me because it is towards evening.

O Lover of men, so lonely, so forsaken, if Your object in staying with us day and night was to win our love, have You not failed? Has it been worth Your while to work miracle after miracle to produce Your Real Presence upon the altar? Have I made it worth Your while to be there *for me?* Jesus, dear Jesus, I bury my face in my hands; I know of no heart more ungrateful, more callous than my own. I have been miserably unmindful of Your Presence here *for me.* I have let self, pleasure, troubles even—anything and everything furnish an excuse for keeping away from You and neglecting You in that sacramental life which is lived here *for me.*

---

1 Mark vi.

# V

## *What Things?*

*"Art Thou a stranger and hast not known the things that have been done in these days?" To whom He said: "What things?"*
(Luke xxiv. 18,19.)

SOME of us, may-be, are deterred from visiting our Lord in the Blessed Sacrament by a false conception of what a visit should be. We suppose that the occupations which fill our heads and our hands from morning till night must all be laid aside at the church door and sternly forbidden entrance, much in the same way as we bid our dog lie down in the porch and wait for us. We read that St. Bernard thus dismissed all secular thoughts, and we conclude—though his biographer does not say so—that they returned at the end of his prayer, *and not before.* Self-mastery such as this demands an effort to which few of us feel equal. Do what they will, the mind of the doctor and the lawyer will run more or less upon their anxious cases, the student's head will be full of his examination, the mother's of her household cares. These thoughts, if indeliberate, will be at least persistent, and if quite deliberate will become sinful. In either case they render prayer an impossibility—hence we stay away.

Now do we find this view of prayer borne out by the practice of God's servants? Of David in perplexity and trouble we read: "And the Philistines coming spread themselves in the valley of Raphaim. And David consulted the Lord, saying:

Shall I go up to the Philistines? and wilt Thou deliver them into my hand? And the Lord said to David: Go up, for I will surely deliver the Philistines into thy hand...And the Philistines came up again...And David consulted the Lord: Shall I go up against the Philistines?...He answered: Go not up against them."[1]

Of David in a mood of joy and thankfulness we are told: "And King David came and sat before the Lord, and said: Who am I, O Lord God, that Thou shouldst give such things to me?"[2]

See, too, the simplicity and confidence of Ezechias on receiving the threatening message of Sennacherib: "And Ezechias took the letter from the hand of the messengers, and read it, and went up to the house of the Lord, and spread it before the Lord."[3]

A common complaint is that daily worries and anxieties so invade our minds that our prayer has no chance. But is this our feeling about a talk with a trusty friend—a man of sound judgment, wide experience and influence, on whose interest in all that concerns us we can count with certainty? Should we say: "I had half an hour with him this morning, but my mind was so full of that affair I could find nothing to say"; or: "I had it all out with him this morning, and am ever so much better already"?

Why not deal thus familiarly with our best Friend? If Ezechias could spread out his letter before the Lord in that old Temple, which was but a shadow of the better things to come, why may not we carry our good news and our bad before the pitying human Heart of Christ, with us all days on purpose to hear every day—and, if we will, every hour of the day—all we have to tell Him, and hearing all, to help in all?

Had our Lord said to us: "I will prosper any spiritual concerns that you commend to Me, but really you must

---

1  2 Kings v.      2  1 Par. xvii.      3  Isa. xxxvii.

look after your own temporal affairs, and I shall count it an irreverence if you bring such things into My presence"—had He said this, there might be some excuse for the pains we take to shut Him out of the cares and business of everyday life.

But has He said this, or does all we know of Him go to prove the exact contrary? Did He count it an irreverence when the sick were thrust upon Him at every step; when a paralytic let down from the roof and laid at His feet stopped His teaching; when messengers came one upon another to draw Him here and there for some temporal need: "Lord, he whom Thou lovest is sick"[1]; "Lord, come down before that my son die"[2]? Did He refuse the invitation at Cana? And if, for a brief space, He delayed the miracle designed from all eternity to manifest His tender interest in the joys as well as in the sorrows of home life, was it not obviously to show how Mary's heart beat in unison with His, and to honour His Mother's prayer?

"Lord, come and see," said the weeping sisters as they led the way to the grave. Look at Him between them, listening now to one, now to the other, as they tell the history of the past three days—how they had watched and waited for Him, and counted on His coming, and He came not. See their tearful eyes. See the eager Heart, longing for the moment when He may reward their trust and turn their mourning into gladness.

What should we have felt and said that day at Bethany if, after raising Lazarus, He had turned to us and made Himself our listener, placing Himself, as was His wont, at the complete disposal of the one who wanted Him? Should we have felt shy of trying to interest Him in the details of our life, in our little joys and troubles? Or would our hearts have opened out to Him, and simply emptied themselves in His presence?

---

1 John xi.      2 *Ibid.* iv.

Do we want an ideal visit to Christ? Let us seek it in Nicodemus' talks by night; in the centurion's urgent pleading for his servant; in the unburdening of soul that we see in Zaccheus and in the sisters at Bethany. And let us frame our own visits on such models. If a big worry threatens to invade prayer, why not take it straight away into prayer, giving it the place and time it wants, making it the subject-matter of our intercourse with God, and so turning a hindrance into a help!

Of course we must do all this with reverence and a certain amount of watchfulness, or our prayer will be no prayer at all, but distraction pure and simple. But if we put our case before our Lord and talk it over with Him, representing our difficulty, asking His advice, listening to His whispered word in answer, our time of prayer will be what He wants it to be—a time of rest, and light, and strength.

Some may say that this so-called prayer is very unsupernatural, and that the results of such a compromise between prayer and distraction will not be very satisfactory. It may be so; we can only reply that there are times without number when this is the only method of getting results at all, and that our Lord's method of dealing with His own and theirs with Him was *eminently natural.*

No, surely, our difficulty is not due to want of sympathy on the part of Christ our Lord. It can only come from our failing to recognise the full purpose of the Incarnation and its bearing on every detail of human life. Had His act of Redemption been His one motive in coming amongst us, He might have come straight from His throne at the right hand of the Father to the cross on Calvary. But the proof of *love greater than which no man can give* did not satisfy Him. He wanted, as "Firstborn amongst many brethren,"[1] as Head of the human family,

---
1 Rom. viii.

to place Himself in intimate communication with it on every side—to touch, as far as might be, every point, every experience of human life, entering personally into its mysteries of joy, and fear, and love, and sorrow. And so we have the years of infancy and childhood and youth, and—precious above all—the blessed years of the public life, when "the Lord Jesus came in and went out among us,"[1] proving by every word and act His desire to be associated with us His brethren, His right to His name of predilection—*the Son of Man*.

He it is Whom we find waiting for us when our turn comes to pass across the short stage of life on earth. He calls us to Him, calls us by our name, one by one. He bids us take Him to our hearts as the nearest and dearest of our friends, Who alone can stand by us when all others fail. He bids us cultivate His friendship, and try it and prove it. And He promises that we shall find Him what all have found Him who have put their trust in Him—what Martha and Mary, and Paul and Bernard, and Teresa and Margaret Mary have found Him—the "Faithful and True,"[2] "Jesus Christ yesterday, and to-day: and the same for ever."[3]

---

[1] Acts i.     [2] Apoc. xix.     [3] Heb. xiii.

## VI
## *Venite ad Me Omnes*

(Matt. xi. 28.)

"Come to Me, heavy-laden ones, come all!"
    I hear, I rise, I hasten at His call;
'Neath burden bent, across the threshold steal,
The curtain lift, and in His Presence kneel:
      There loose my load—and wide,
        With none to check nor chide,
    Scattering, a sorry sight, on every side,

They fall—pains, troubles, cares—lying, how meet,
About the weary, way-worn, wounded Feet;
Under the Eye of yore bedimmed with tears,
The Heart Gethsemane oppressed with fears,
      The Heart that sore afraid
        Strong supplication made,
And with a sweat of blood the Father prayed.

Beneath His glance, as snow 'neath sunny ray,
Some of my cares dissolve and melt away,
And some He takes and smoothes a little space
The less to chafe, and lays again in place.
      'Tis mystery to me
        How some He smiles to see,
And how on some His tears fall tenderly.

One I hold up to Him, and pleading pray,
"This, Lord, just this, in pity take away!"
And ever comes His word with cheering smile:
"A little longer, trust Me yet awhile;
    Each pang of keen distress,
    Each prayer, I mark and bless,
Each in its hour shall show forth fruitfulness".

*That*, my life's woe, against a bleeding Side
Is pressed, and lo! transfigured, glorified,
It glows as crystal flushed with rosy ray.
"O gem unprized! Restore it, Lord, I pray;
    As costly gift from Thee
    Dear shall it be to me";
And in my heart I hide it lovingly.

A lightened load He lays on me, all sweet
With words of love—and thus I leave His Feet,
With steadier step to plod on day by day,
With stouter heart to climb the upward way
    And when anew life's strain
    Frets me with weary pain,
I take my load and go to Him again.

# VII

# *The Hidden God*

*Vere Tu es Deus absconditus!*
(Isaias xiv. 15.)

THERE is no use denying that with the exception of rare intervals, our intercourse with God in this life is more or less laborious and difficult. This is only saying that Heaven is not yet come. Faith was meant to be a trial, and a trial it certainly is. The evidence of sense is against us; the levity of imagination is against us; the inconstancy of our desires and of our will is against us when we kneel down to pray.

"Behold He standeth behind our wall."[1] We know He is there, close as the priest in the confessional, with attention to every word we say. Yet, for all that, the words and the confidences come slowly. It is hard to prolong a conversation that is all on one side, and this, so it seems to us, is the case in prayer. Useless to tell us that our faith is at fault. That in the presence of the Pope, or the King, we should be all attention. Where the conditions are so different, there can be no parallel. The voice, the look, the question and answer, the surroundings—all these are wanting. Such admonitions irritate us by their injustice, and we look away wearily for help elsewhere. But where to look? We cannot alter the present state of things or fix our wandering thoughts and unstable heart. No, but we can accept all things as they are in truth, and in the truth find a remedy.

---

1  Cant. ii.

"Behold He standeth behind our wall." But the barrier between us is not a drawback, an obstacle to union with Him—inseparable indeed from the present condition of things—yet an obstacle for all that. It is distinctly willed by Him as a necessary part of our trial, a wholesome discipline, a purification of love. It has in it all the privileges, advantages and blessings that in this life belong to pain, and can be won by pain alone. It is a present blessing as well as a pledge of blessing to come. "Blessed *are* they that have not seen and have believed."[1] It is a pledge of that full clear vision, "reserved in heaven for you, who, by the power of God, are kept by faith unto salvation, ready to be revealed in the last time. Wherein you shall greatly rejoice, if now for a little time you must be made sorrowful...That the trial of your faith (much more precious than gold tried by the fire) may be found unto praise and glory and honour at the appearing of Jesus Christ: Whom having not seen you love; in Whom also now, though you see Him not, you believe, and believing shall rejoice with joy unspeakable."[2]

"We see now in a dark manner: but then face to face."[3] "I shall see Him, but not now."[4] How will that face to face vision be the brighter and the sweeter for the dimness now! How will the joy of that moment when we part for ever with faith be intensified by what faith has cost us in the past!

> O days and hours, your work is this,
>    To hold me from my proper place,
>    A little while from His embrace,
> For fuller gain of after bliss.
> That out of distance might ensue
>    Desire of nearness doubly sweet,
>    And unto meeting when we meet,
> Delight a hundredfold accrue.
>               —*In Memoriam*

---

1 John xx.     2 1 Peter i.     3 1 Cor. xiii.
4 Numbers xxiv.

## VIII

# *Looking Through the Lattices*

(Cant. ii. 9.)

BUT meanwhile the Beloved *is* behind the wall. And He is there with all the sympathy for our difficulty which His perfect knowledge of it enables Him to have. "Jesus...needed not that any man should tell Him...for He knew what was in man."[1] He knows the weariness of praying on against apparently unanswered prayer; against the pain of physical restlessness, the labour of thought, the irksomeness of concentration, the perpetual gathering together of the forces that are playing truant in a thousand fields, recalled for a brief space only to be off again more wayward for their capture. All this He knows. And our remedy is to remember that He knows it. He Who has appointed prayer to be the channel of grace, means *such prayer as we can bring Him*. He does not ask impossibilities. He does not place us amid distracting work all day long and expect us to shut it out by an effort of will the moment we kneel down to pray. Nor even to shut it out by repeated efforts. He would have us turn our distractions and weariness not so much into matter for self-reproach, or humiliation even, as into a loving, trustful plea for His pity and His help. This is prayer. Lay the tired brain, the strained

---

1   John ii.

muscles, the aching head—lay them all down at His feet without a word, just for His eye to rest on and His Heart to help and heal.

There are times when physical lassitude, cold or heat, an importunate thought, a trial with its sting still fresh, baffles every effort to fix the mind on the subject of prayer, and concentrates the whole attention on what for the moment is all-absorbing. Times harder still to manage, when mind and heart are so absolutely vacant and callous that there is no rousing them to action. This reflection will sometimes be helpful then: What should I have to say were I in the presence of the one I love best in the world; with whom I am quite at my ease; my friend *par excellence*; to whom my trials, difficulties, character, the secrets of my soul are known; that one in whose concerns and welfare I take the deepest interest; whose plans and views are mine, discussed again and again together; in whose company time flies and the hour for parting comes too soon—what should I find to say?

Say it, make an effort to say it to Him Who is in the tabernacle yonder.

O Jesus, hidden God, more friendly than a brother,[1] I believe most firmly that You are present, a few feet only from where I kneel. You are behind that little wall, listening for every word of confidence, and love, and thanksgiving, and praise. Listening when my heart is free to pour itself out to You as the brook to the river in the days of spring. Listening more tenderly when the stream is ice-bound; when I kneel before You troubled, wearied, anxious about many things—about many souls perhaps—yet dry and hard, without a word to say. Make my heart so perfectly at ease with You, O Lord, that it may be able to turn to You even in its coldness and inertness;

---

[1] Prov. xviii.

to confide to You naturally all that most intimately concerns it; to be content with this, when discontented with all else, with self most of all—that You know all men and need not that any should give testimony of man, for You know what is in man.¹

---

1   John ii.

## IX
## *Lord, Come and See!*

(John xi. 34.)

Come to my heart as unto Bethl'hem's grot,
A hovel-home that love despises not:
Can love transform it to a pleasant spot?
    Lord, come and see!

Come to my heart as once to Bethany:
A brother's grave is there, and piteously
Are tears and supplication calling Thee:
    Lord, come and see!

How flocked of yore unto Thy blessed feet
The sick, the sad, Thy mercy to entreat!
I too have needs Thy pitying eye to meet:
    Lord, come and see!

Come, lay Thy hand upon each leprous stain;
Come with Thy word of might the fiend to chain;
The open festering sore, the hidden pain,
    Lord, come and see!

Come to my heart, this dull cold heart of mine,
All irresponsive to a love divine;
What lacks it to become Thy hallowed shrine?
    Lord, come and see!

Happier by far than in the olden days
Judea's glorious Temple—what delays
Its song and sacrifice, its prayer and praise?
   Lord, come and see!

Perchance, like Temple Courts, doth sinful stain,
The world's loud trafficking, the greed of gain
Thy Father's house, the house of prayer profane:
   Lord, come and see!

Come, Holy One, I yield myself to Thee;
E'en scourge in hand, come, Lord and Love, to me.
What change shall make me Thine, Thine utterly?
   Lord, come and see!

# X
# *Neglect*

*He came unto His own, and His own received Him not.*
(John i. II.)

How strange it seems, O Lord! For You had been promised so long. You had been so ardently desired by the best and noblest of our race; so gloriously prefigured, so set forth in prophecy, as to awaken the keenest expectation and enkindle the most glowing love. How was it, then, that Your own received You not? How is it that even now You come unto Your own and are not welcomed, are not wanted, are left alone, not through the night only—that perhaps were to be expected—but through the long day hours, with Your so-called friends, and the weary and the heavy laden within a stone's throw of Your door? Ah, Lord, the outrage and the sacrilege that mark the hatred of Your enemies are less to be wondered at, less to be deplored, than the coldness of those You call Your own. You are not given to complain. But when along the ages a meek remonstrance does break upon the silence, it is always the same—the protest wrung from You by the desertion of those You love. "*Behold...my familiar friends also are departed from me...My brethren have passed by me.*"[1] "*Do you now believe? Behold...you shall be scattered every man to his own, and shall leave Me alone.*"[2] How Your Heart felt the desolation of abandonment; how, to speak human language,

---
[1] Job vi.  [2] John xvi.

You feel it still—You made known in that cry of unrequited love, "Behold this Heart which has so loved men and is so little loved by them."

Who would have thought that God could upbraid so tenderly, or that men could hear such reproach without being touched and won! If not to make great sacrifices for Him, if not to give up all, at least to go a few steps in order to keep Him company in His loneliness, and sympathise with Him in His sorrows—surely He might have looked for this!

Dearest Lord, one would have expected You to be in such request upon the altar; expected that there would be crowding and crushing in Your presence as in the days of Your earthly life; that we should be seen flocking to You early and late, to show our appreciation of Your love, and to pour out our troubles into Your willing ear. Where is our faith to leave You thus deserted? "Do you believe? Behold you shall be scattered every one to his own, and shall leave Me alone."

*He came unto His own*—that is, He comes as far as He can—from heaven to the Host, and down to the altar rails. Further He cannot come. The rest of the way must be ours. We must meet Him there in Holy Communion, or His loving journey to us will have been in vain. He will not force our free will. But He does so want to come. Shall we disappoint Him? Oh, if our own love will not draw us to Him, at least let us have compassion on His! If we think ourselves at liberty to deprive ourselves of our communions, surely we are not free to deprive Him of His.

You long, O Lover of my soul, to come to me. Your delights are to be with me, cold, inhospitable as I am. Come, then; come, Lord Jesus, and in satisfying Your own desire, enkindle mine.

# XI
# *Faith*

*Sola fides sufficit!*

WHAT mainly hinders the freedom and happiness of our intercourse with Christ our Lord in the Blessed Sacrament is the account we make *of feelings*. In spite of all that can be said to us, we persist in applying this untrustworthy test to our relations with God, the result being discouragement and all its evil consequences.

Feelings are wayward children, all the more refractory often for blandishments and coaxing. Our wisest plan is not to notice them overmuch; to be glad certainly when they show themselves friendly, and when they are unpropitious to let them alone.

Feelings we may dispense with, but faith never. Faith we must follow, lean upon, cling to, with all the more tenacity as the days draw on of which our Lord said: "The Son of man when He cometh, shall He find, think you, faith on earth?"[1] With the vehemence that will take no refusal we must constrain her, saying: "Stay with us, because it is towards evening."[2] Where faith enters and takes full possession, all good things enter with her. We need not go about to seek anxiously for anything else: *Sola fides sufficit!*

---

1  Luke xviii.         2  *Ibid.* xxiv.

Give me, my God, a deep and lively faith in all Your Holy Spirit has revealed and Your Church teaches. Give me this one thing necessary, and it is enough for me. *Sola fides sufficit!* The faith I ask is a living faith that must needs prove its vitality by good works. Give me the faith that lit up the lives of Your saints. Strengthen my hold on all revealed truth. But give me above all an intense, ever-growing realisation of the mystery of the altar, the central Mystery of our faith.

Realised by me as it was by Your saints, what a change that Presence would make in my life! Mind, heart, imagination, will, views, aims, desires directed to it, absorbed by it—O Jesus, what a transformation this would be! *Sola fides sufficit!* Lord, increase my faith!

>Thou Who of old didst love Thy hand to lay
>    On the dull, vacant eyes that craved for light,
>Behold, I come to Thee, and crying, pray:
>    O Christ, O Son of David, give me sight!
>A faith scarce clouded by the mists of earth,
>    A faith that pierceth heaven I ask of Thee,
>Faith to prize all things by their lasting worth:
>    Thou canst, Thou wilt—O Lord, that I may see!

If we would think more about arousing our faith than exciting our feelings, would not our visits and our communions be the gainers? And would not the affections of the heart often follow the lead of faith? A few minutes spent in trying to bring home to ourselves that He Who is really present a few yards from where we sit or kneel is the world's long-promised Messiah, Whose advent kings and prophets desired to see; Whom in His own time all men desired to see and hear; He at Whose feet Mary sat at Bethany, unmindful of all but that Face and that Voice; He Whose words—"Peace, be still," "Thy brother shall rise again," "Go, and now sin no more"—brought hope and joy to the troubled heart; He Who fell on His Face under the olive trees, crushed to the earth by my sin; Who died with the thought and the love of me in His Heart that Good Friday long ago; Who is to come again in the eastern sky where every eye shall see Him—a few minutes of earnest dwelling on thoughts such as these will rouse in our souls faith and hope and charity, will kindle humility, sorrow, gratitude, desire—for fuel is furnished for the fire.

"Lord, I believe, help Thou my unbelief." I believe that beneath Your humble veils You are here truly present, O hidden God! I believe the day draws near when You will be the hidden God no more; when I shall see You coming in the clouds of heaven with great power and majesty, all nature trembling at Your approach; whilst the elect lift up their heads because their redemption is at hand.

O Judge of the living and the dead, in that awful day remember me! Remember me when You come to gather Your own into Your kingdom! Remember, I beseech You, in that second coming, how often I have welcomed You at Your hidden coming, and let my heart welcome and leap up to meet You then.

*Jesu, quem velatum nunc aspicio,*
*Oro, fiat illud, quod tam sitio,*
*Ut, Te revelata cernens facie,*
*Visu sim beatus Tuae gloriae.*

O Jesu, Whom by faith I now descry
  Shrouded from mortal eye;
When wilt Thou slake the thirsting of my heart
  To see Thee as Thou art,
Face unto face in all Thy glad array,
  'Tranced with the glory of that everlasting day.

—G.T.

## XII

## *After a Defeat*

*Let not this thing discourage thee, for various is the event of war.*
(2 Kings xi. 25.)

THE cheery words You have for me, O Lord and Leader, when downcast and troubled I come to tell You of another reverse to our arms! Truly Your ways are not our ways. With us results are everything. A general may do his best, take every precaution, be skilful in preparation, and brave in action. Yet repeated mishaps will beget mistrust, and he will find himself superseded in command. It must be so. But it is not Your way with us.

I have not done my best. I have been careless in preparation, and weak and cowardly in action. Yet You have nothing but encouragement for me after a rout. No reproach, no withdrawal of confidence: "Fight like a good soldier; and if sometimes thou fall through frailty, rise up again with greater strength than before, confiding in My more abundant grace."[1] At my first call for help reinforcements are sent to the front—not *less*, by reason of my unfaithfulness, but *more*, because of my need. And if I am superseded in command, it is only by Your coming Yourself on to the field, and so strengthening my hands, that all must give way before us.

I am sorry, O my Chief, for the dishonour to Your name and the loss to Your cause through my fault. But I do not

---
1 *Imit. of Christ*, iii. 6.

despond. I may fail in everything else, but in trust I will never fail. If I am overthrown seventy-seven times in the day, I will return to the charge as often, my resolution the same, my confidence the same as at first. These perpetual beginnings are painful, weary work, but Your patience, Lord, will never fail: neither shall my goodwill. I know that the struggle itself brings You glory. I know that if I keep up the struggle to the end, You will meet me when the time of trial is over with the welcome word: "*Well done!*"

> Fearful of self, with sore temptation pressing,
>    I hasten, God of armies, unto Thee,
> My every power, my every sense confessing
>    Its insufficiency.
> Taught by the past there is no help in me,
>    I cast myself on Thee.
>
> This is not hard. But false in face of Heaven,
>    To turn with trusting heart again to Thee,
> Not once, not twice, but seventy times seven.
>    In brave humility:
> When smarting self would hide its misery,
>    To cast myself on Thee—
>
> Lord, *this is hard*. Thine eye alone can measure
>    The weary pain of each relapse to me:
> Yet fraught with grace, all stored with hidden treasure,
>    Is my infirmity;
> Strongest of pleas, the creature's frailty,
>    That casts it upon Thee.

# XIII
# *After a Victory*

*Thanks be to God, Who hath given us the victory through our Lord Jesus Christ.*
(I Cor. xv. 57.)

So often, dear Lord, so very often I come to You with my defeats, that it is a refreshment to have something more cheering to offer to Your Sacred Heart.

*Thanks be to God*—It was Your grace, my God, throughout—before, accompanying, crowning—my share just the co-operation that did not reject the help You gave.

*Who hath given us*—given *me*, so weak, so cowardly, so little to be depended on in moments of trouble and conflict; *me*, such a disgrace to the colours often, such a sorry soldier at best—

*The victory*—nothing much for anyone else, but something of a triumph, dear Lord, for me. Our small successes are not accounted small by You, O generous Leader. You welcome all, are proud of all, lay up reward and praise for all against the day of reward.

*Through our Lord Jesus Christ*, by Whom, with Whom, in Whom we overcome. We can do all things in Him Who strengthens us. *Jesu, Tibi sit gloria!* Thanks be to God, Who has given us the victory through our Lord Jesus Christ.

## XIV

## *A Divine Friend*

*The woman...came and fell down before Him, and told Him all the truth.*
(Mark v. 33.)

THE *whole truth.* Only to one Friend can we tell that. Only one friendship could bear the strain of that revelation. The very exigencies of other friendships call for restraint. Can we own to want of confidence, to utter coldness and callousness, to a want of sympathy in joys and sorrows that move to its depths the heart of our friend? Could the most self-forgetting of human friendships bear up against avowals such as these?

No; we must draw the line here unless we want the free flowing waters gradually to freeze into a glacier. Owning to mistrust will hardly be accepted as a mark of trust, nor will the acknowledgment of coldness beget love. Poor affection of these human hearts of ours!—jealous and suspicious at the least show of reticence, yet unable to bear the disclosures of unreserve. We cannot be hard upon a weakness common to us all, but we long for a heart human like our own, yet strong enough to support the weight of all we would put upon it. Nor are we disappointed. Here in the tabernacle is what we seek. Here is a Heart waiting for all, ready for all. Here we may unbosom ourselves completely. Here we may tell *the whole truth.* Narrowness and fickleness, heartlessness, mistrust, selfishness—ingratitude even, we may tell. We may trust all to this Beloved without fear. For He knows what is in man. No revelation will surprise Him, no misery disgust Him. He will welcome each painful avowal with the tenderest sympathy, and take all we tell Him as tokens of trust for which He is infinitely obliged to us.

## XV

## *An Evening Visit*

*Stay with us, because it is towards evening.*
(Luke xxiv. 29.)

IT IS at night especially that the shepherd looks well to his sheep. Good Shepherd, I gather round You to-night the sheep of Your world-wide flock and commit them to Your keeping. Wherever they are to be found, there are You in the midst of them. In crowded cities—the guardian of the multitudes sleeping around You on every side. In the one spot of the quiet village where a light will burn to-night—the Keeper of the simple souls around You there. In many a hut the wide world over—content among savage tribes to share the poor shelter of Your priest. Everywhere warding off the prowling wolf and the evil that walketh in the dark.[1] With us not only all days, but all nights unto the end of time.

*Stay with us*, Lord, to-night. Stay to adore, and praise, and give thanks for us whilst we sleep; to draw down mercy and grace upon the world; to succour from earth's tabernacles the holy suffering souls in purgatory in their long night of weary pain.

*Stay with us*, to ward off the anger of God from our crowded cities with their dens of vice, their crimes that call to Heaven for vengeance.

---
1 Psa. xc.

*Stay with us*, to guard the innocent, to sustain the tempted, to raise the fallen, to curb the power of the evil one, to prevent sin.

*Stay with us*, to comfort the sorrowing, to bless the death-beds, to grant contrition to the dying, to receive into the arms of Your mercy the thousands that this night must come before You for judgment. O Good Shepherd, stay with Your sheep! Secure them against the perils that beset them. Stay, above all, with the suffering and the dying. "Grant us a quiet night and a perfect end." Be our merciful Shepherd to the last, that without fear we may appear before You as our Judge.

*Stay with us, Lord, to-night.* More favoured than the camp of Israel slumbering under the guardianship of the pillar of fire, we sleep with the Presence of God Incarnate shielding us on every side. Well may we say: "In peace, in the self same, I will sleep and I will rest."

"Vouchsafe, O Lord, this night to keep us without sin."

I map out the whole world into districts, and place each under the jurisdiction of the nearest tabernacle. From that centre let the radiance of the Divine protection go forth to every soul within its circuit, enlightening, guarding—above all, strengthening against sin. O Lord, from every tabernacle send forth to-night a strong efficacious grace, to stop not one but a thousand sins. Because we have made the Most High our refuge,[1] let no evil come near to hurt us. "Save us, O Lord, waking, and keep us while we sleep, that we may watch with Christ and rest in peace."

---

1 Psa. xc.

# XVI
## *Privileged*

*My lots are in Thy hands.*
(Psa. xxx. 15.)

SUPPOSE, my God, You had told us that as we know the worth of our soul, You were going to trust us with the choice of the means by which its salvation is to be worked out; You were going to put before us riches and poverty, sickness and health, success and failure, a long life and a short one, and we might take which seemed best for us. Should we be content? Should we not say, if we were wise: "My God, do not trust this to me. I shall choose, I know I shall, what I like, not what is best for me."

And suppose You were to tell us there were souls to whom You would not entrust such a decision. Either they were too weak, or You were so anxious to save them that You had left the choice of means, not to themselves, but to those who love them better than they love themselves, and who would choose for them more wisely—to their guardian angel, to their patron saint, even to the Seat of Wisdom herself—and if we wished You would let us be one of those favoured souls. Should we be content then? Or should we say: "My God, forgive me for being mistrustful still. I know my guardian angel and my holy patrons, and most of all my Mother Mary, love me dearly and would do their best for me. But their wisdom after all is not infinite. They might make a mistake, and that mistake might mean the loss of everything to me. I cannot afford any risk here. My soul is my only one; I must save it whatever happens. I dare not keep it in my own hands, and I dare not trust it even to the highest and holiest and wisest of those around Your throne."

And suppose once again You were to say to us: "There are a few, a very few, whose salvation is so dear to Me that I will trust the choice of means to no one. I will plan and arrange all Myself. Nothing shall happen to them but what has been foreseen and prepared from all eternity by My Infinite Wisdom and Goodness. No one shall touch them; no joy nor sorrow shall come in their way—no, nor a hair of their head fall to the ground without My knowledge and permission." Should we not cry out: "My God—I hardly dare to ask it; but, oh, that I might be one of that happy chosen few, for surely they are safe!"

You check me by a warning: "These souls will not have all their own way in life. Their road will sometimes be hard and rugged. They will see things prosper in the hands of others and fail in theirs. They will be hardly used by those around them —misjudged, set aside, unjustly treated; life to many of them will be uphill work." Do I draw back now, or do I cry out again: "No matter that, oh, no matter that at all! What will they care when they know Your arm is round them as they go uphill; Your hand sends the cross and the failure and the pain! No, my God, that does not frighten me. Let me only be one of those whose lot is altogether in Your hands, and I will fear nothing; I will complain of nothing; nay, I will be grateful for all that comes to me. I will kiss Your hand even when You strike me. I shall feel peaceful and happy always in the thought that it is the wisdom of my God that orders all for me, and the love of my heavenly Father that provides everything to help me. Let me be one of those chosen ones, and You will see how I value my privilege, how I prize whatever You send."

*Suppose*—I have been saying. But this is no supposition. I am that privileged one whose life in its minutest details is Your ordering and Your care. How can I complain, my God! How can I be mistrustful or even anxious—"My lots are in Thy hands."

## XVII

# The Improvidence of Love

*My thoughts are not your thoughts, nor your ways My ways, saith the Lord.*
(Isa. lv. 8.)

How often I kneel here before the tabernacle and make my genuflection and my act of faith without realising in the very least what I believe, what I adore. How little I heed that where I stand is holy ground. That a few paces from me lies the most mysterious of all mysteries, "the mystery of faith," the mystery of love—love that with infinite wisdom and infinite power at its service has here reached its limits, has found bounds which God Himself cannot overpass.

And yet *is* the Eucharist after all the greatest of mysteries? Has it not its source in a deeper mystery still? Is anything wonderful after the Incarnation? Does not the marvel of God made Man outstrip all other marvels? If the Creator, out of love for man, must needs annihilate Himself so far as to assume a created nature, where will such love stop? Into what further extravagances of love will it not be betrayed?

But how was it, my God, that Your infinite wisdom did not fear the consequences of such prodigality; did not remember who those are with whom You have to deal; did not consider that too great lavishness blunts the edge of our appreciation and our gratitude? Had You taken counsel of us, O loving Lord, we should have bid You in the very interests of love not to overdo its manifestation, not to make Yourself too easy of access, lest familiarity should endanger reverence. Daily Communion; the easy, easy conditions on which You come to us; the tarrying day and night in every church throughout the world—this we should have said would bring about a contempt of these sacred mysteries and deprive You of the love which is the end of their institution. You would have had to own to the justice of our remonstrance, to acknowledge that such fears were well grounded. It was not safe to ask counsel—except of Your own Heart. "Who hath known the mind of the Lord? and who hath been His counsellor?"[1] Only His Heart. O Sacred Heart, how sadly You have laid Him open to every sort of indignity—to indifference, coldness, outrage, sacrilege. Yet, in spite of all, this Gift of God is without repentance,[2] "for My thoughts are not your thoughts, nor your ways My ways, saith the Lord."

---

1  Isa. xl.         2  Rom. xi.

## XVIII

## *Changes*

*Behold, I make all things new!*
(Apoc. xxi. 5.)

How easily changes come about under Your hand, O Lord! Noiselessly, almost unnoticed, every hour of the day and night, all the world over, the most stupendous change is taking place—the change of the lowly substance of bread into Your Sacred Body, of wine into Your Precious Blood.

So is it in the world of souls. The most marvellous transformations cost You but a word. *Follow Me!* And instantly apostle after apostle leaves all and follows You— mind, heart, views, ambitions, the whole aspect of life changed. *Saul, Saul, why persecutest thou Me?* And he who had "beyond measure persecuted the Church of God"[1] rises to his feet ready to carry the name of Jesus "before the Gentiles, and kings, and the children of Israel."[2]

With a word You can change *me*. The apathy for spiritual things would go—the dullness of sight, the slowness of heart, the low aims, the weak desires, the feebleness in the conflict with self, the niggardliness in Your service—all these would go. You could draw me within Your attraction; You could make me follow You, not simply through duty or interest, but with

---

1 Gal. i.      2 Acts ix.

the quick step of one to whom Your service is the absorbing interest of life. You could make Yourself so much the need of my soul that it would turn to You as the flowers to the sun for warmth and colour, for growth, for beauty, for its very life. With a word You could work a change such as this. And what is there to hinder it? You are there in the tabernacle, O Sun of Justice, near enough to warm me through and through with Your heat; and oh, how often—did I only desire it—You would come still nearer, entering my very heart to make it live by You!

Say the word that You desire to say more than I to hear. Speak, Lord, for Thy servant heareth. Say the transforming word each morning over my heart when You stand at the altar and say it over the bread and wine. Say the word that will change the lowliest, the vilest thing of earth *into Yourself.* See my heart, see the hearts of all I love upon the paten, awaiting there Your creative word. Change them from what they are to what You would have them be.

# XIX

# I Have Somewhat to Say to Thee

(Luke vii. 40.)

A WORD to me? a word for me apart
No other ear to hearken—heart to heart?
A word Thy hidden pleasure to impart?
    O Master, say it!

Is it a word of love, entreating mine—
Poor recompense indeed for love divine,
Yet precious to that human Heart of Thine?
    Dear Master, say it!

A word of blame? Lord, I deserve it—nay,
No word of Thine can I deserve—yet may
I know what chiding love would have Thee say?
    O Master, say it!

A word to cast aside my craven fears,
And bravely bear the cross these many years
Dragged after Thee with protest and with tears?
    O Master, say it!

Perchance a dreaded word, not once or twice,
But often suing for a gift of price;
Can I invite that call to sacrifice?
    Yes, Master, say it!

A word from Thee the rightful course will trace,
A word from Thee the shrinking spirit brace,
A word from Thee bestow all needful grace,
    O Master, say it!

No word of Thine but gives before it takes,
And taking, generous compensation makes,
And effort asking, energy awakes,
    O Master, say it!

A warning maybe—frighted love's disguise,
How stern soe'er in seeming, kindly wise,
Unveiling danger to unwary eyes?
    O Master, say it!

Thy voice is ever music to mine ear,
Silence alone o'erwhelms my soul with fear
Say all, say freely what I crave to hear,
    O Master, say it!

One tender word to Thomas brought belief,
One pitying word, a kingdom to a thief,
One only word would bring my soul relief,
    O Master, say it!

New shape would aims, desires, affections take,
New power of sacrifice within me wake,
New need of toil and suffering for Thy sake,
    O Master, say it!

One word, I know, Thou hast for me—a word
In the still hours of prayer how often heard,
Not long, perchance, its welcome sound deferred,
    O Master, say it!

Word life's incessant prayer must wrest from Thee;
Word holding my eternal destiny,
Word I must hear or perish utterly,
    O Master, say it!

When past my little day of time and grace,
Lone in another world I seek my place,
And trembling fall before Thy unveiled Face,
    Dear Master, say it!

*Come!*—blest recall from exile's weary years,
Rest from the awful strife 'twixt hopes and fears,
Sweet word of welcome after toil and tears,
    O Master, say it!

Though silent now, keep Thou that word in store,
The word to make me Thine for evermore;
By all Thy loving-kindness, I implore,
    Dear Master, say it!

## XX
# *A Divine Plaint*

*My people have done two evils.
They have forsaken Me, the fountain of living water, and have digged to
themselves cisterns, broken cisterns, that can hold no water.*
(Jer. ii. 13.)

WHAT heart so hard but could find a motive for contrition in this tender reproach! No question here of the Divine majesty outraged, the Divine rights infringed. The harm *to ourselves*—this is the evil we have done by forsaking God. And He stands sadly by, watching our futile efforts to fill with earth's sorry pleasures the hearts created for Himself.

The plaint is echoed by the Incarnate Son. "*You will not come to Me that you may have life.*"[1] And echoed not once, nor from Jerusalem only, but through all time and from the countless tabernacles where the Eucharistic Life is being lived for us. How is it that that cry does not arrest us as we go heedlessly on our way? What a difference it would make to our round of daily toil and worries and anxieties if we carried away oftener from the altar the Life Who is waiting there to give Himself to us. He would not encroach upon our time. He is the most considerate of guests, and knows we are no more able to lay aside our domestic cares than was His own blessed Mother in her little cave-home at Nazareth. He would not

---
1 John v.

interfere with our projects, our occupations, our amusements even. But He would act the part of a helpmate throughout, guiding our plans, sanctifying our work, ennobling our pleasures—above all, sharing and soothing our sorrows. Is an ally such as this so easily found that we can afford to turn a deaf ear to the invitation from the tabernacle: "Whom seekest thou—a friend? I am He."

O Loving One, who are we that You should so earnestly entreat our friendship? Have You not thronging about You legions upon legions of angels? What need can You have of us? Yet You not only tolerate our society but beg for it. The little troublesome children whom strangers find a nuisance are a solace to the father, who feels something to be missing unless he has them pressing and chattering all about him. So is it with You. To satisfy Your Heart You must have us, needy and clamorous, all about You, besetting You on every side.

Lord, had we always treated You as You deserve, could You be more in love with our company? Surely Your eagerness should drive away fear that our uncouthness and coldness will disgust You. Love "is patient, is kind,...beareth all things,... hopeth all things, endureth all things."[1] O Lord and Lover, we will not disappoint You. Since You are content to have us as we are, we will draw near to You without fear: "Behold we come to Thee; for Thou art the Lord our God."[2]

---

1  I Cor. xiii.         2  Jer. iii.

## XXI

## *Thanksgiving*

*And he fell on his face before His feet, giving thanks.*
(Luke xvii. 16.)

JUST as I do to-day, dear Lord, in the fulness of my heart, in the first transport of joy and praise and gratitude that comes with the sense of answered prayer. My happiness is all from You. In all that has happened I trace the workings of Your hand, and see how it has moved all secondary causes, and ordered all things sweetly.

"Thou, O my God, hast made me joyful with great joy."[1]

"Blessed be the Lord God this day."[2]

"We bless Thee, O Lord God, because it hath not happened as we suspected. For Thou hast shewn Thy mercy to us, and Thou hast taken pity."[3]

"Bless the Lord, O my soul, and let all that is within me bless His holy name. Bless the Lord, O my soul, and never forget all He hath done for thee...Who satisfieth thy desire with good things...The Lord is compassionate and merciful... He hath not dealt with us according to our sins...The mercy of the Lord is from eternity and unto eternity upon them that fear Him."[4]

"Give glory to the Lord, for He is good: for His mercy endureth for ever. Let them say so that have been redeemed

---

1  *Cf.* 2 Esdras xii.    2   3 Kings v.    3   3 Tobias viii.
4  Psa. cii.

by the Lord, whom He hath redeemed from the hand of the enemy...They cried to the Lord in their tribulation, and He delivered them out of their distresses...Let the mercies of the Lord give glory to Him and His wonderful works to the children of men. For He hath satisfied the empty soul, and hath filled the hungry soul with good things."[1]

"Praise ye the Lord, for the Lord is good; sing ye to His name, for it is sweet."[2]

"Who healeth the broken of heart, and bindeth up their bruises."[3]

"The Lord hath granted me my petition which I asked of Him."[4]

"Blessed be God, Who hath not turned away my prayer, nor His mercy from me."[5]

"O Lord our God, all this store ... is from Thy hand."[6]

"O Lord, there is none like Thee."[7]

*He fell on his face before His feet giving thanks.* The right place, the right posture for thanksgiving. My whole self, body and soul, seeks to pour itself out in praise. And yet, my God, when do we feel ourselves more helpless, more bound in by our narrowness than when we come to thanksgiving! Our heart is freer on the path of sorrow than on that of joy. It knows its way better. It can go further. There are novenas of Ten Fridays, Masses and Communions, year after year of persistent prayer. But when the answer comes at last; when suddenly the burden is lifted; when the thrill of gladness and the stillness of peace succeed one another in sweet alternations within the soul—how poor, how soon ended is our *Te Deum!* A rush to Your feet—a few tears perhaps—a few broken words of gratitude,

---

1  Ibid. cvi.
2  Ibid. cxxxiv.
3  Ibid. cxlvi.
4  I Kings i.
5  Psa. lxv.
6  I Par. xxix.
7  Ibid. xvii.

and—our heart fails us. In vain do we lift it up in David's heart, that censer of glorious praise. There weighs upon it still the stifling sense of oppression. We can but sink back in our helplessness and long for the full freedom of all our powers that is to come.

Oh yes, the soul never feels so powerless, so imprisoned as when the call upon it is for thanksgiving. It is a caged bird always, but it never beats more hopelessly against the bars than when it would soar upward in the free flight of praise.

It is then we turn to our God with us on the altar, to the Victim of infinite worth placed at our disposal to be offered to God as a full, worthy, adequate return for all His goodness to us.

"What shall I render to the Lord for all He hath rendered unto me?"

I will come to the altar of God to unite my thanksgiving and my praise with the divine gratitude of the God-Man.

I will offer with Him His sacrifice and mine, a gift of infinite value from my grateful heart.

I will receive into my poor heart, whose powers, stretched to their utmost, fall infinitely short of what is due to Him, the Heart of the Man-God.

My God, I rejoice beyond measure that in Mass and Holy Communion I can offer You a thanksgiving that is adequate because infinite, a thanksgiving worthy of Your acceptance. Look not on the poverty of my praise, but "look upon the Face of Thy Christ."[1] *Per Ipsum, et cum Ipso, et in Ipso...omnis honor et gloria. Amen.*

---

1 Psa. lxxxiii.

## XXII
# *Darkness*

*My God, My God, why hast Thou forsaken Me?*
(Matt. xxvii. 46.)

My God! as if You belonged to no one else in the wide world. As if You and I were alone in creation. As if neither in heaven above nor in the earth beneath, nor in the waters under the earth, You had a single other creature!

*My God!* as if for me alone you had done all in the orders of nature, grace, and glory; working for me from the beginning, through all causes, by all creatures, in all events. As if for me alone were the earth and the sea and all within them. For me all the ordering of Your Providence in the affairs of time. For me the heaven of heavens and all the concourse there. For me the Saints and Mary; the Incarnation, the Life, and death, and teaching of Christ; the Church and Sacraments; the Eucharist, and Mass, and Communion. For me life everlasting and the Blessed Vision of Yourself.

*My God!* for Whom I am made. Without Whom happiness for me were the wildest of impossibilities. The Supreme Good able to satisfy to the full every want of my complex nature. Infinite Goodness providing for all and for each with an exquisite discrimination of my need.

*My God!* in a sense known to myself and You alone— father, mother, sister, brother, lover, friend—all in all to me.

*My God!* as if You belonged to me rather than to Yourself; belonged to me rather than I to You. As if You were for my sake rather than I for Yours. Or at least as if we so belonged to one another as of necessity to imply and supplement each other—as hill and valley, light and shade, the ocean and the void it fills.

*My God, my God, why hast Thou forsaken me?* Why this darkness in which I grope for You in vain, in which I seek in vain to find Your Face? Why these nameless fears, this dread of You, this shrinking from You?

Or—harder still to bear—this heaviness of soul, this hardness of heart, this weariness of You, my God, this restlessness in Your presence, this impatience of Your ways—why all this inconsistency and perversity?

Why, O Supreme Good, do You show Yourself to me as infinitely desirable, only to elude my grasp when I stretch out my hands to feel for You and draw You to myself? Why do You brush past me in the darkness to leave me all the more desolate and disconsolate because You were so near? Why are You deaf when I cry? Why, here in this tabernacle, are You so near and yet so far away? Why do You make it more and more impossible for me to find rest out of You, and then deny Yourself to my soul? Why have You sought for me so persistently when I fled from You, to hide from me now that I seek You? *My God, my God, why hast Thou forsaken me?*

Is Your answer to me this—that I have forsaken You first? Is the hiding of Your Face the just punishment of wilful deafness to Your voice and resistance to Your leading? Are You waiting for some act of mine as the price of Your turning to me? Is it pride or any other passion that interposes as a cloud between us? What is it, my God? Take it away at any cost. I am sorry for my insincerity; for all meanness in my dealings with

You; for all wilful blindness and deafness; for the cowardice that fears to see what will call for effort and for sacrifice.

If conscience does not reproach me, I am not hereby justified, because Your all-seeing eye may note, does note what escapes mine. I own to whatever You see that is amiss. I am perfectly conscious that there is more—oh, a thousand times more than enough to make You turn away Your Face and forsake me utterly. Show me what You will have me see, that I may amend it, and bear with what You dare not show me, lest I should be utterly cast down and despair.

*My God, My God, why hast Thou forsaken Me!* You have taught me by Your own meek complaint that I too may complain lovingly. I look up through the darkness of Calvary. I hear above me that cry from Your own lips, and I am instructed and comforted. If the well-beloved Son, for bearing the appearance of sin, was thus shut out from the Father's Face, how shall a sinner complain? If this was done in the green wood, what shall be done in the dry?

And if all through the blackness of that desolation He remained still the well-beloved Son, so may the weakest of His brethren, so may I remain—dear to the Father's Heart through all the discipline of chastisement, through all the needful purification of my imperfect love.

In the very midnight of His dereliction He called on the Father, clung to the Father, threw Himself on the Father with absolute trust. So may I, so *must* I, in the darkness that is but the faintest shadow of His.

Father, into Thy hands I commend my *spirit*—for this trial, for every trial, for the last trial, when the shadow of death will close round me, and it will be hard to find Your Face. Into the hands that created me, that redeemed me, into which I shall pass at the moment of death, Father, into Thy hands I commend my spirit.

"My God, My God!"—into the night went forth
    That lonely cry,
Piteous as never plaint from burdened breast
    Its misery.

Went forth *for me* into the night, that wail
    Of woe divine;
His bitter dereliction bared, to draw
    The sting from mine.

And yet another cry ere shades of death
    Around Him stole,
Revealed the sanctuary dark and lone
    Of Jesu's soul:

"Father, into Thy hands"—a Son's bequest,
    That we might know
The filial, all unshaken trust, beneath
    That depth of woe.

"Father, into Thy hands"—that we might learn
    Since Jesus died
Theirs first the right to claim the Father's love,
    His crucified.

## XXIII
# *"What is Truth?"*

(John xviii. 38.)

"PILATE saith to Him: What is truth? And when he said this he went out."

Too often, O Lord, in my dealings with You I am like Pilate. Moved by Your grace to desire the things that are for my peace, I come to You to know my way: *"What shall I do to possess everlasting life?"*[1] *"Make the way known to me, wherein I should walk."*[2] *"Teach me to do Thy will, for Thou art my God."*[3] And when I have said this I go out. I do not wait to hear an answer which may exact more of me than I am prepared to give. I am afraid to remain in Your Presence, lest You should beckon whither I am not willing to follow. And so I ask lightly: "What is truth?" without waiting to hear what the Lord my God will speak in me.[4]

How much more readily I pray for light than for strength. *"Lord, that I may see!"* And when the scales begin to fall from my eyes, I turn away lest I should find what I am seeking.

It is not Your way, O Lord, to constrain our free will. You meet us half-way, more than half-way by a great deal. But You have decreed that further and more abundant grace—the grace that is efficacious—shall be the reward of correspondence. If we withhold this, we enter upon a terrible contest between

---
1 Luke xviii.   2 Psa. cxlii.   3 *Ibid*.
4 Psa. lxxxiv.

Your invitation on the one hand and the shrinking of nature on the other.

"Pilate saith to Him: What is truth? And when he had said this he went out again to the Jews and said to them: I find no cause in Him...Then Pilate took Jesus and scourged Him... And went forth again and saith to the Jews: Behold I bring Him forth unto you that you may know that I find no cause in Him... Take Him you and crucify Him for I find no cause in Him...The Jews answered: He ought to die because He made Himself the Son of God. When Pilate therefore had heard this saying he feared the more. And he entered into the hall again and said to Jesus: Whence art Thou? But Jesus gave him no answer. From thenceforth Pilate sought to release Him...And he saith to the Jews: Behold your King...Then he delivered Him to them to be crucified."

Oh, the agony of mind, the risk, the misery we bring upon ourselves by our vacillations and trifling with grace! Surely the remedy is to gain, by prayer, strength proportioned to the light God gives. It is as easy for Him to give the one as the other, for "there is none strong like our God."[1] But I must ask, for "strength cometh from Heaven."[2] "Ask and it shall be given to you." "God is my strong One, in Him will I trust...my rock, and my strength, and my Saviour."[3] He will not leave me in my weakness. If He shows me His ways, He will give me strength to walk in them. "My God is made my strength."[4]

---

[1] I Kings ii.   [2] I Mach. iii.   [3] 2 Kings xxii.
[4] Isa. xlix.

## XXIV

## *His Second Coming*

*They shall see the Son of Man coming in the clouds of heaven...
and then shall all the tribes of the earth mourn.*
(Matt. xxiv. 30.)

DEAREST Lord, is there a sadder word than this in the whole of the written Word? Did a sadder ever fall from Your sacred lips? That when You come again to finish the work of redemption by the destruction of the last enemy, death; to gather to Yourself those for whose salvation You came down from heaven, and were incarnate, and suffered, and died, and founded Your Church, and gave Your sacraments; those whom You bade to watch and wait for You and lift up their heads at Your coming; that when at last You come, this shall be Your reception—"*then shall all the tribes of the earth mourn!*"

What an awful testimony to the decay of truth among the children of men, to the unchristianising of the world! "*All the tribes of the earth*" as if the elect would be but as the ears of corn left on the field after the harvesting. O Messiah, so long promised, so earnestly expected—is this the return of those to whom You were sent, among whom You have lived as one of themselves, for whom You have sacrificed everything You took from our nature?

"*They shall see the Son of Man coming*"—not now in the midnight silence as once to Mary, not hidden under lowly accidents as through long centuries upon the altar, but "in great power and majesty," "the King in His beauty," revealed to every eye. *"And then shall all the tribes of the earth mourn."*

The awfulness of these words must have struck the Twelve as they sat about Your feet that day on Olivet looking down upon Josaphat, for John re-echoed them from Patmos half a century later: "Behold, He cometh with the clouds, and every eye shall see Him...And all the tribes of the earth shall bewail themselves because of Him."[1]

How our hearts would sink within us were it not for those other words equally with these the words of truth: "He shall send His angels to gather together His elect from the four winds, from the uttermost part of the earth, to the uttermost part of heaven."[2] From every corner of the earth will those blessed ones come trooping in—"a great multitude, which no man can number, of all nations, and tribes, and peoples, and tongues."[3]

Lord Jesus! Who would not desire with desire to be one of that great multitude, were it only to console Your Heart for the losses of that day! Let this happiness be mine, and that of as many as can be reached by the utmost stretching of Your mercy, the fullest and farthest flowing of Your precious Blood!

> *Quaerens me sedisti lassus,*
> *Redemisti crucem passus:*
> *Tantus labor non sit cassus.*

Have mercy, O Lord, on all the tribes of earth, that they may not perish, nor bewail themselves because of You when You come to judgment. Have mercy, that when the day of the Lord, that dreadful day shall come, the number of the elect may be multiplied, and the thirst of Your Heart appeased.

---

1 Apoc. i.      2 Mark xiii.      3 Apoc. vii.

# XXV
## *Our Earth*

*Coeli enarrant gloriam Dei.*
(Psa. xviii. 1.)

THE *heavens declare the glory of God.* There are hours when the grandeur of the midnight skies draws from our hearts: "*Coeli enarrant,*" and conversely: "*Quam sordet tellus!*" "How vile earth appears when I look up to heaven!"[1] When we would wish to be so far away from earth, so near to God, that we could cover it with our two hands and shut it out, with all its sinfulness, from His sight.

And there are hours when we re-echo David's other cry: "*The earth is the Lord's.*"[2] Studded with millions of stars—its sanctuary lamps—here in grand constellations, there in solitary beauty amid the darkness, it lies outstretched before its Creator, a very heaven. Yes, speck as it is in creation, our world has a beauty all its own in the eyes of Him Who made it. "There is not found the like to it in glory." Marred and sin-stained, it is still the dear world of the Incarnation, the world God so loved as to give to it His Son. Its highways, its fields, its waters have felt the tread of His feet; to the end of time He has made it His home. "I have chosen and have sanctified this place, and My eyes and My heart shall be there always."[3] Always. His interest in it is as keen—as human—as when, a wayfarer here,

---

1   St. Ignatius.        2   Ps. xxiii.        3   2 Par. vii.

He shared its joys and sorrows. Its every man, woman, and child to-day has a distinct place in His heart.

His sacramental Presence sanctifies it from pole to pole. On each of its altars a divine sacrifice is offered day by day. In each of its tabernacles is gathered up the worship of all creation. From each an unceasing praise goes up to the Throne of God, infinitely transcending the paltry outrages of man. From each radiates a divine life, communicating itself to all the members of the Body of Christ. From each, as from a well-spring, go forth all graces of light and strength; all holy impulses and high resolves; all courage, steadfastness, perseverance in well-doing; all works of love to the members, born of love to the Head. All spiritual energy, from the robust virtue of the saint to the weakest supernatural act of the repentant sinner, is flowing this hour from earth's countless tabernacles, giving to God a glory before which the material glory of the starry heavens pales into insignificance.

O hidden God, I adore You as the source of all this glorious life. Who would not love the world, which You have so loved as to make it Your home all days even to the end of time? Who would not strive with You and for Your sake to light up its dark places, to cleanse its foul places, to spread far and near the saving knowledge of its Redeemer, that so the love poured out upon it, the Blood shed for it, may not have been in vain?

What can I do, O Lord, within my narrow sphere, to help on the coming of Your Kingdom in the world? What have You given me to give away again in Your service? As to what do You say to me: "Freely have you received, freely give?"[1] Is it health, wealth, talent, influence, leisure for good works in any of the various fields calling for my aid and open to me? Is it devotedness and self-sacrifice in the apostolate of home life? Or is it the noblest and most far-reaching of works for God: the

---
[1] Matt. x.

training of young souls in His love and service? Am I doing good work for You in my allotted sphere? What account am I preparing to give You of the talents entrusted to me? How could I bear it, O my Lord, should You ever have to reproach me, as "an evil and slothful servant," with hiding the talent given me for Your service? What am I doing with my life, with its energies, its opportunities, its responsibilities, its graces? Where are the souls I am helping to save? Where is the lot I am brightening, the cross I am lightening for Your dear sake? In what direction am I furthering Your interests and sacrificing self to Your glory? Unless I can lay my hands in Yours, and look up trustfully into Your Face with "Lord, Thou knowest" my daily prayer, "Thy Kingdom come" is a mockery, a self-delusion, a sham.

# XXVI

## Christ Our Study

*You have not so learned Christ.*
(Ephes. iv. 20.)

It behoves us to have right conceptions of the great spiritual realities which affect our life here and our destiny hereafter. Above all must we learn aright Him Who is the Way, the Truth, and the Life. Gradually, from our earliest childhood, the idea of Christ has been forming, developing, taking definite shape in our minds. Maybe it is stereotyped by this time. It is all-imperative for us that the Christ we have so conceived should be the true Christ—"the Christ, the Son of the Living God." *Tout sort des idées.* Our idea of Him will not affect Himself or alter our fundamental relations with Him, but it will affect the whole moulding of our spiritual life, our whole character, our every thought, word and deed here, and our whole eternity hereafter. Surely, then, we must examine our impression of Christ, and should we find that the influence of early education, of a false creed, of unwholesome reading or association, or the trend of our character has distorted in our minds the true Christ as reflected in the Gospels, we must at all costs correct that impression. If it has become stereotyped we must break up our mould and start our work afresh.

Meditation upon the Gospels; the quiet, steady gaze of the inward eye on Christ; the study of Him day after day under all circumstances and amid ever shifting scenes—and not of His outward bearing, His words and actions only, but of the Heart from which these spring—thus it was that the saints built up His image in their souls, a true living image which transformed them into the likeness of itself, and became a power within them, drawing all things to Him Who was to them all in all.

*You have not so learned Christ.* If Christ our Lord has not as yet drawn *me* wholly to Himself, it is because my conception of Him is faulty. Whether this is the result of simple carelessness which has allowed His image in my mind to take shape anyhow, or of Jansenistic habits of thought that have fashioned for me a Lord stern, exacting, repellent—a very caricature of the Christ of the Gospels, Christ our Lord; or whether it is my own character—timorous, suspicious, selfish, unsympathising—that has inspired my present idea of Him; from whatever source the misconception has come, it must be set right, or its results will be simply fatal—fatal to the growth of anything like personal love and familiar friendship with Him; fatal to His influence on my life, my actions, my work for Him in the souls of others.

Not any Christ, the creature of my own distorted fancy, but Him Whom the Father has sent, I am to fall down and worship. He alone has power, as He alone has right, to occupy and absorb my whole interest, my whole affection, my whole self. He alone can be a living influence radiating from my own life to the lives of others.

O Christ my Lord, give me so to know You that my knowledge may be glory to You, and life to my own soul and the souls of others. "This is eternal life: that they may know Thee, the only true God, and Jesus Christ, Whom Thou hast sent."[1] Be Yourself my Master in this one thing necessary. And let me go to the source to draw—learning You from the scenes

---
1  John xvii.

of Your life. Let me stand by the well of Samaria, and the pool of Bethsaida, and the bier at Nain—and watch and listen. Let the charm of Your divine Person subdue and win me, and the sound of Your voice be familiar to me. Let the knowledge of Your ways with the sinner, the sufferer, the little children, grave such a picture of You in my heart that not even its perversity can bring before me when I say "Jesus" any other form than that of the most beautiful, the most tender, the most compassionate of men.

Veronica wiped Your sacred suffering Face, and received as the greatest of rewards, stamped on her veil, and still more upon her heart, that *vera icon*—that true image of Christ which was thenceforth to be inseparable from her memory, the very name by which all ages were to know her.

Stamp on my heart, dear Lord, *the true likeness* of Yourself. And as this likeness must be ever growing, let me come often to the altar rails to learn You more and more. The tabernacle is the Gospel history continued. Time has not dimmed Your fairness, O beautiful One, nor dulled the sympathy of Your human Heart. All that You were to Your own in this world, all that You are to them this hour in heaven, is here within the tabernacle, is here *for me*. Here then let me come to study You—patient, tender, obedient still, meek and humble of heart, Jesus, yesterday, to-day and for ever!

## XXVII

# *Our Father*

*O clap your hands, all ye nations; shout unto God with the voice of joy.*
(Psa. xlvi. 1.)

MY GOD, what would have become of us had You shown Yourself to us as the All-just instead of the All-loving One You are? Had You been more mindful of Your Majesty than of our need? We know so little how to comport ourselves in Your presence, that it might have seemed more fitting You should remain in the recesses of Your Godhead, manifest Yourself but dimly and rarely, and restrict our worship of You to the most distant homage. It would have been but the manifestation of another attribute in place of that sweet mercy which has shaped the whole course, not of redemption's plan only, but of the inner life of each one of us.

My God, it might have been so—and what then would have become of us? Where would praise have been, and trust, and loving return to Your arms after a fall? Blessed be Your name that You willed to show Yourself our Father, willed that with the younger race, Your human family, mercy should ever be in the ascendant.

"*Blessed be You for ever, my God, my Mercy,*"[1] for having shown Yourself to our weak sight in this softened light, the light that begets love—as One easily appeased, as One constraining trust, as One with arms widespread to Your timid children—the All-forgiving, All-tender, All-compassionate—*our Father Who art in heaven.*

---
1   *Cf.* Psa. lviii.

## XXVIII

## *Hereafter*

*Thou knowest not now, but thou shalt know hereafter.*
(John xiii. 7.)

I LOOK forward into the eternal years and see myself at last in my rest on the bosom of God. All over! Life, and uncertainty, and death, and judgment, and purgatory. And with my head on the Heart of Him Who has loved me to the end, I look back. How clear everything is from this height, in this unclouded light and this untroubled peace! All mists swept away; all doubts dispelled; all questions set at rest; all cravings satisfied.

*Thou shalt know hereafter.* Why that persistent prayer remained unanswered; why evil prospered and good was overcome; why in spite of every effort those difficulties remained difficulties to the last—how plain it all is now! I see now the everlasting results of the thoughts, and words, and acts that sped so quickly by. I see the distinct work of each in shaping my eternity, I see the relation of grace to glory; why I enjoy the blessed vision of God thus far and no farther. Where I guided my steps by the light of faith, clung to God in the darkness, "joined myself to Him and endured"—what fruit of joy for eternity! Where there was cowardice, self-seeking, above all, mistrust of God—what loss that can never, never be repaired! Oh, why did I not realise that I was meant to live by faith during my little life down there, in order to enjoy the fruits of faith in this real life of eternity!

*Thou knowest not now, but thou shalt know hereafter.* But I *may* know now if I pray for light and strength. I may know now the things that are for my peace. I may have now the spiritual insight, the *lumen cordium* which the Holy Spirit gives to all who ask.

Lord Jesus, here really present, make me see now by the light of faith what I shall see almost directly in the light of eternity; when I look back on life, and grace, and sacraments, and opportunities, on worldly aims and worldly honours—from my place in heaven. By the tears You shed over Jerusalem that knew not the day of her visitation, grant that I, that all I love, that all men may know in this our day the things that are for our peace.

> Dawn now—the hours of earth's expectancy,
> From the grey heaven enough of light to guide
> The wary feet—no more; enough to trace
> Against the sky in outline faint and blurred
> Fair forms, their fairness shrouded for the nonce:
> In every line of grace and symmetry
> And tender hue to be revealed, when day
> This hazy scene shall flood with living light,
> Bathing all things in beauty. Now we know
> In part, the noontide comes and *we shall see.*

> O restless heart! resenting mystery,
> Angry with night, that by Divine decree
> Divides with day the task of perfecting
> God's world of souls—fret not against the gloom
> That, baffling, humbles thee. Why this reverse,
> This wrong defeating right, brave effort crowned
> By failure, good with itself at variance,
> Thou know'st not now; *now* the strong trial of faith,
> The clinging, blind with tears, unto thy God
> In patient trust—*hereafter thou shalt see.*

## XXIX

## *My Vineyard*

*Let us see if the vineyard flourish.*
(Cant. vii. 12.)

THE vivid lightnings of the East that reveal in all the brightness of day what lay hidden in darkness, have their parallel in the flood of light flashed at times upon the soul. Without warning, without apparent cause, it comes—a momentary brightness, but lasting in its effects. Imagination, mind, heart—all have been steeped in it; henceforth the truth it has lit up becomes a force to influence our life here and our eternity hereafter. Has our responsibility to others been ever thrust upon us in one of these bursts of light? Have we realised, as it were for the first time, the influence which, in God's inscrutable designs, we have over the destiny of others; the dread power which—wittingly or unwittingly, for good or for evil—we are ever exercising over those around us; the account which will be demanded of such a trust?

O God, You have given "to every one of us commandment concerning our neighbour."[1] What kind of influence has mine been thus far? At the sixth, the ninth, the eleventh hour it was said to me: "Go you into My vineyard."[2] What has been the result of that call and of that mission? There has been a corner of that vineyard marked out for me to tend. Am I labouring in it with earnestness, with self-sacrifice, with the purity of intention

---

1   Ecclus. xvii.          2   Matt. xx.

that overcomes difficulties, and survives disappointment, and is undisturbed by failure, because it looks to You alone, works not for self but for Your glory? Or am I slumbering at my post? With what feelings do I hear You say to me: "Let us see if the vineyard flourish, if the flowers be ready to bring forth fruits!"[1] Is it of me You say: "I passed by the field of the slothful man, and by the vineyard of the foolish man. And behold it was all filled with nettles, and thorns had covered the face thereof, and the stone-wall was broken down?"[2] Must I own in my shame, "My vineyard I have not kept?"[3]

O Lord of the vineyard, Whose love and trust are shown in this, that You have called me to labour for what is dearer to You than Your very life—how have I justified Your trust? Do not punish my slothfulness by making over to another's more earnest toil what has been given into my care. But rather stand by and help me to work according to Your will, that nothing may perish or suffer loss through fault of mine. Help me to watch vigilantly the little plot committed to me; to cast out carefully all noxious weeds; to dig, to prune, to bind up and strengthen what is weak; "in solicitude not slothful, in spirit fervent serving the Lord."[4] Then shall my vineyard flourish and bring forth fruit to Your glory in due season.

---

1  Cant. vii.  2  Prov. xxiv.  3  Cant. i.
4  Rom. xii.

## XXX

## *Where We Are True*

*Thou sayest, I am rich, and made wealthy, and have need of nothing: and knowest not, that thou art wretched, and miserable, and poor, and blind, and naked.*
(Apoc. iii. 17.)

IT SEEMS to me, dear Lord, that You can hardly reproach me with this. I know but too well how deficient I am in humility; how I fire up at even a hint implying blame, suspicion, mistrust; how reluctantly I own to those about me that I am in the wrong.

But alone with You, my inward witness, it is otherwise. There is no difficulty, no reluctance here. Once in the Presence Chamber, the curtain dropped behind me, the gaze of creatures turned aside, I am myself, *and true*, without disguise, feint, tricking out of any sort. I do not trim my speech, or tone down my "*Peccavi*," "to make excuses in sins."[1] I conceal neither my failings nor my needs. With the privilege of the creature in presence of the Creator, I lie on my face before You just as I am, for Your eye to see, Your ear to hearken to, Your Heart to pity and to bless.

How could there be pretence with You or affectation? I know and feel that "Thy eyes are upon me,"[2] "beholding the good and the evil;"[3] that "God Who seeth all"[4] "is the weigher

---

1  Psa. cxl.  2  Job vii.  3  Prov. xv.
4  Ecclus. vii.

of spirits."¹ Before that all-seeing Eye self-delusion, conceit, untruthfulness in every shape must melt away.

I cannot indeed know my nothingness and sinfulness as they are known to You. I do not fathom one of the thousand motives I have for self-abasement in Your sight. But I think my self-knowledge as far as it goes is true. I am ready to see with You that I am wretched and miserable and poor and blind and naked. I know and feel with the most intimate conviction that in my soul are the seeds of every evil passion; that they will choke the good seed and ruin me unless Your power represses them; that unless Your Almighty hand checks the weight of temptation, my enemy must prevail over me; that it is owing to Your goodness I have not been tempted as others; that of myself I am nothing but weakness and misery and sin.

How it comes to pass that my self-knowledge does not bear better fruit; that when occasion requires I am not more ready to own to what I am thus conscious of, am not more indulgent and compassionate in my judgment of others—I know not. But I thank You for what You have given; and ask earnestly for more and stronger light to bring about conformity between my interior conviction and my exterior words and actions.

*Veni, Pater pauperum,*
*Veni, Dator munerum,*
*Veni, Lumen cordium.*

---

1 Prov. xvi.

## XXXI
## *In Silence and in Hope*

(Isa. xxx. 15.)

S HE came with her crushing memories,
    She came with her secret fears,
She brought Him her hidden misery
    And her bitter burning tears.

And all alone at that cheerless board
    Prepared Him her own sweet feast,
Offering her heart with her spikenard
    And the kiss that "never ceased."

She marvelled when He upbraided
    The cruel thoughts of men,
And tears fell fast as He lauded her—
    Her, Mary Magdalen.

As she marked how His Heart no token
    Of her contrite love had missed,
The love that had given of its best,
    Anointed, and washed, and kissed;

And tendered a heart with penitence
    Filled to the very brim,
And braved the scorn of a carping crowd
    To stake its all on Him.

## In Silence and in Hope

Absorbed in her loving ministries
    She knelt at His Feet apart,
The scandal of every eye save one
    That soundeth the secret heart.

She knew that her unforgiven past
    Lay open to His ken,
Yet no word of supplication,
    Spake Mary Magdalen.

Love taught a sublimer pleading,
    Elected a better part—
Calm trust in Him Who spurneth not
    The humble contrite heart.

From out the fulness of His own
    Came plenary release:
"Her many sins are pardoned her:
    Arise and go in peace."

O Christ, Who that poor sinner's love
    So gloriously hast crowned,
That through all time her name with Thine
    Shall through the world resound;

Who waitest here the penitent,
    All-pitying now as then,
Give me the brave, unfaltering trust
    Of Thy dear Magdalen.

## XXXII
## God's Work

*To the Lord was His own work known from the beginning of the world.*
*(Acts xv. 18.)*

WERE Your work known to us, my God, as it is to You, how well ordered our minds and hearts, our views, affections, lives would be! How all things would fall into their proper places—events public and private, every detail of Your Providence affecting ourselves and others! Our desires especially—how tranquil, how subordinated they would be! Or, rather, would there be any desire save for the furtherance of Your work by the fulfilment of Your will?

But may not this be our disposition now by means of faith? May we not see in all that happens the action or the permission of God, to Whom His own work is known?

A child in the midst of a crowd is conscious of nothing but its immediate surroundings. Crushed and stifled, it can see and feel only the objects actually touching it. But let the father take it up in his arms and hold it aloft—what a difference the elevation will make!

I am in a crowd; in the dark, with the narrowest views and interests; knowing but dimly for what we are come together; finding no meaning often in what is stirring around me. But should God deign to raise me to His point of view, what a change would come over me! How differently I should look on all things! In all that happens I should see the good pleasure or the permission of His Providence: "reaching from end to end mightily, and ordering all things sweetly."[1] This would not dull my susceptibilities, nor cramp my desires. Far from it! With the widened prospect, interests would multiply on every side. But all things would be seen in their true light. In all I should recognise the Divine will unfolding itself in the course of events, and guiding all things, undeterred by the action of man's free will, to its own predetermined ends. In a deadly contest involving my country's honour and welfare, my patriotism would run high. But too violent regrets at the reverses of our arms, too vehement anxiety as to the issue, would be held in check by my ignorance of God's designs. Once known by the issue, His will would be accepted loyally, simply because it was His will. "Thanks be to God, Who hath given us the victory."[2] Or—in spite of human feeling and repugnance—"The Lord gave, and the Lord hath taken away: blessed be the name of the Lord."[3]

So in family trials, the hidden sorrows of the heart, the vicissitudes of the spiritual life—there would be the habit of looking up into my Father's Face to see His meaning in it all; and where I could not see, learning to bow my head and kiss His hand. "Yea, Father; for so hath it seemed good in Thy sight."[4]

Does the Creator ask too much of His little creature when He bids it submit itself thus to Him? Or is it not rather a marvellous condescension on His part to invite the fusion of our will with the Divine, thus associating us with Himself in the work known to Him from the beginning?

What You want, my God, You shall have, and as cheerfully as I can give it. To give without cost or pain is not always in my power. You do not ask this: nay, You accept the cost and pain

---
1 Wisd. viii.    2 I Cor. xv.    3 Job i.
4 Matt. xi.

as proving greater love. You value above all things the faith that gives in the dark, not seeing Your open hand, nor the smile which would be its instant reward; not understanding as yet the joy our fidelity is to Him Who deigns to realise His eternal designs through the instrumentality of our free will.

O God, let not mine be wanting! Take all I have—take it at any cost. I make You welcome to all. My reward shall be to kneel at Your feet one day, and follow Your finger, showing how, here in brightness, here in shade, Your work was entrusted to me, and—my God, what joy! I have not disappointed You.

## XXXIII

# *A Strong Cry*

*They rebuked him, that he should hold his peace.
But he cried out much more: "Son of David, have mercy on me."*
(Luke xviii. 39.)

THERE are moments when we fling ourselves before the Tabernacle with a desire too vehement for words. These translate our thoughts and needs up to a certain point. Beyond that, we must betake ourselves to the cry of the heart.

What a relief to know that that cry passes instantly into the presence of Him Who made us, and is welcomed there. Nay, it has not even a presence-chamber to seek, for "He is not far from any one of us."[1] "His ear lies ever on our lips." And this is yet too far. As the sponge in mid-ocean, so are we borne up, environed, penetrated, saturated with Him. "In Him we live and move and have our being."[2] This is He to Whom we cry. Nor need we even cry. For "all things are naked and open to the eyes of Him to Whom our speech is."[3] Our God is nigh unto us; He is within us; more present to us than we are to ourselves. He knows the need that casts us on our face before Him. He saw our trouble before it took shape in our soul. He knows each thrill of pain, and the agony of helplessness, and the fear that holds us as in a vice. All this He knows. And He is not displeased with the passionate earnestness of our cry for help. Job was blameless before God when his misery forced from him bold words of expostulation. Jacob was

---

1  Acts xvii.        2  *Ibid.*        3  Heb. iv.

blessed for being strong against God. Our Almighty Father loves to be overcome by His children. He is willing to have His gifts wrested from Him by the intensity of prayer. Nor will He have such prayer to be disconcerted or turned aside by the evidence of its untimeliness. No, not even when He ignores or denies it. He loves the trust that catches up the rebuff and flings it back, a passionate plea for mercy:—

"It is not good to take the children's bread and to cast it to the dogs."[1]

"Yea, Lord; for the whelps also eat of the crumbs that fall from the table of their masters."

Oh, that I had this strength of purpose, this trust that sweeps all before it! Here on the altar I have my model in prayer—Him "Who in the days of His flesh with a strong cry offered up prayers and supplications[2]: *Abba*, Father, all things are possible to Thee, remove this chalice from me, but not what I will, but what Thou wilt."[3] "And being in an agony, He prayed the longer."[4] "And He prayed the third time, saying the self same word."[5]

Our prayer can never be too urgent, too persistent, if only we kneel by Your side and follow Your lead, O Lord. We may return again and again upon the same plea: *Abba, Pater, omnia Tibi possibilia sunt*. All things, all things are possible to Thee; take this chalice from me. Yet—for Thou knowest best, and I am shortsighted and self-seeking, and know not the things that are for my peace—*not my will, but Thine be done*. Let that will be done which in a little while, when I look down upon this trial from the unclouded brightness of my place in heaven, I shall joyfully own to have been for the best, better a thousand times than anything I could have devised. "Father, if Thou wilt, remove this chalice from me. But if this chalice may not pass away, but I must drink it, Thy will be done."

---

1 Mark vii.     2 Heb v.     3 Mark xiv.
4 Luke xxii.     5 Matt. xxvi.

## XXXIV

## *"Be Ready!"*

*(A visit for the First Friday of the month.)*

"BE *ready!*" Your word of warning, Lord, and my one desire. And so I come to You to get ready.

I shall be too weak and suffering on my bed of death, too appalled by the sight of my past life to be able to do much by way of preparation for the Last Sacraments. Yet I shall need all their grace, and I must bring to them at least the necessary dispositions. Take the care of all upon Yourself. See Yourself to my dispositions. Look upon all as a trust committed to You long ago, committed to You again and again with the more self-abandonment as the time and circumstances of my last hour are absolutely unknown to me. Let me find out in that hour how well it is to have hoped in the Lord. Let me find You, my Lord, in death equal to Yourself—to all I have found You in life.

And when the hour for Sacraments has passed; when the Church has stretched her hand to the utmost to hold me to the last, up to the very confines of that world where her jurisdiction stops; when my soul is passing beyond the reach of that hand which has stayed me up till then, and been help and healing all my life through—then, O my Saviour, do for me immediately, by Yourself, what You have done for me through Your Church. Hear Yourself my last confession made straight to Your Heart. Hear my last avowal "of my so many sins"—of those for which I have sorrowed most bitterly, which have been brought oftenest under the absolving hand of Your priest. When my last words in this world are said; when my eyes are closed to the crucifix, and my hands can grasp the rosary no longer; when my ears are shut to all the sounds of earth, and all things are sinking round me—then let me feel You near. Inspire Yourself my last cry for mercy. Sweep away the clouds that will gather thick and fast before the eyes of my soul, seeking to hide that mercy from me. Let Your hand hold me. Let Your arm be round me when all else is falling away. You have passed, O Lord, through the agony of death: be with me in my agony. All the nameless terrors of that hour are known to You. All the dangers that await me then are clear to You here in the tabernacle—the weakness, the weariness, the pains of spirit, and of sense, the temptations kept for the last, the loneliness, the unsuspected snares, the lack of human help. O human Heart, be my secure refuge in that awful hour. I call upon You now to fulfil in my favour then the promise to those devoted to Your sacred Heart: "I will be their assured refuge in life and more especially at death."

*Recordare, Jesu pie,*
*Quod sum causa Tuae viae*
*Ne me perdas illa die.*

*Quaerens me sedisti lassus,*
*Redemisti crucem passus:*
*Tantus labor non sit cassus.*

Recollect, O love divine,
'Twas for this lost sheep of Thine
Thou Thy glory didst resign.

Sattest weary seeking me,
Suff'redst upon the tree:
Let not vain Thy labour be.

## XXXV
## *"Domine, Ecce quem Amas Infirmatur."*

(John xi. 3.)

How many Bethanies, Lord Jesus, have there been in the world since the day You stood with Martha and Mary by the grave of Lazarus! How many there are at this hour! And each with all its pain is known to Your pitying Heart. Every detail known—the fear, the anxiety, the weary yet unwearied prayer, the long, long waiting for Your coming; the hope that rises and falls and clings the faster for its less foothold to Your promises, Your mercy, Your dear human Heart. You know it all. You have seen all, heard all for years. And still You wait, just as You waited beyond the Jordan whilst the sisters wept beside their brother's bed, beside his grave.

"Now Jesus loved Martha, and her sister Mary, and Lazarus. When He had heard therefore that he was sick, He still remained in the same place two days."[1] Why, Lord, why— with Your heart so tender and Your arm so strong, and danger near, and time short, and those You love so fearful and so sad? Why did you still remain, O Lord?

Truly Your thoughts are not as our thoughts, nor Your ways as ours. Our love stands sentry round its dear ones, to ward off pain or sorrow: "Far be it from Thee, Lord, this

---
1  John xi.

shall not be unto Thee."¹ Your love, seeking rather to sanctify than to spare, assigns to sorrow a definite work in behalf of Your beloved. "Whom the Lord loveth, He chastiseth, and He scourgeth every son whom He receiveth."² "Now Jesus loved Martha, and Mary, and Lazarus. When He had heard therefore that he was sick, He still remained in the same place two days."

"Our Lord Himself was perfected by His passion."³ And in that passion it was not the nails which tore the flesh, but the anguish which rent the spirit, that drew forth His bitter cry. It was the passion of His Heart that was the hardest. It is by the crucifixion of the heart that Christ is perfected in us. Therefore He stays away and leaves us to suffering harder far to bear than physical pain. We cry out. We send our messages to Him. And He does not come. "My God, My God, why hast Thou forsaken me!" He hears and does not come. The echo of His own cry of desolation moves His Heart. And still He does not come. It is because Jesus loves that He does violence to His heart and lets the cross do for His friends what it alone can do. This is His way of showing love. He expects us to understand it.

In the cross, as in the sacred mystery of the altar, His love puts on strange disguises. But puts them on so regularly, so frankly, that losing by this time their power of disguise, they ought to reveal instead of hiding Him.

We must be patient and wait. The time of His coming, with its ways and means, we can leave to His wisdom and His love. Our work is to send urgently and perseveringly the message whose trust vanquished His Heart at last and made Him say, "*Let us go to him.*"

"*Lord, behold, he whom Thou lovest is sick.*" Before a thousand tabernacles that cry is rising. No prayer, but pleading more potent than any prayer. Its perseverance is its power.

---

1 Matt. xvi.        2 Heb. xii.        3 Heb. ii.

"*Domine, Ecce quem Amas Infirmatur.*"

Can it but hold out, ignore neglect, support delay, it is sure to hear in God's own time: "Thy brother shall rise again...Lazarus, come forth."

Listen, Lord Jesus, to that cry. By the pity it woke in Your sacred Heart—listen! By the tears You shed with the weeping sisters—listen! Not for one Lazarus only, but for each and every one throughout the world, do we entreat You: *Domine, ecce quem amas infirmatur!* If a miracle is needed, we ask it with confidence. Is there one You would work more gladly? O Lord, make haste to help us. To-day, to-day—to-morrow, perhaps, it will be too late. *Ecce quem amas infirmatur!*

## XXXVI

## *After a Death*

*And his disciples came and took the body, and buried it, and came and told Jesus.*
(Matt. xiv. 12.)

POOR disciples! They had lost their master. Life lay a blank before them; all its meaning gone, all its purpose changed. The support on which they had leaned was taken away—what was to become of them?

Poor disciples indeed—yet happy too. For the hand that dealt the blow held the remedy. It led them to Jesus. What does that mean but that all they had lost was made up to them a thousandfold?

They took the body, and buried it, *and came and told Jesus.* We can see Him receiving the forlorn little band. We can hear His words of tender pity and comfort as He drew them out and got from them all their troubled tale. We can feel the relief it was to tell Him all; feel the peace that stole into their hearts as He spoke to them of their master, and gently won them from their grief, and drew them to Himself. They yielded to the divine attraction of that Eye and that Voice, to the irresistible sympathy of that Heart, to the grace that spoke to their own hearts. And thus that bitter loss proved the crowning grace of their lives, the cause of their eternal joy— because they let it lead them to the feet of Christ— because *they came and told Jesus.*

## After a Death

O Master! I too come to Your feet to tell You all. I have buried my dead. I have lost what can never be restored to me in this world. I have come from the grave with half myself buried there. I have come back to a life with all its meaning gone from it—a life without joy, interest, anything to which my soul responds—a dreary waste stretching before me that I must cross alone. Where shall I turn for courage and for strength? Where but to You, to Whom the disciples of John turned in their desolation? Open to me Your arms and Your Heart. Listen tenderly to me whilst I tell You all my trouble. Speak to my soul and calm it and strengthen it. Make up to me for what You have taken away. And if You ask what compensation I desire, I answer: "None other than Thyself, O Lord."

Let us both be gainers by this bitter loss—You by the fuller surrender into Your hands of all that I have and am; I by the fuller gift of Yourself to my soul—a fulness satisfying its every craving with the love of Him, from Whom neither life nor death, nor things present nor things to come, have power to part me.

## XXXVII
# *God's Ways*

*Wherein hast Thou loved us?*
(Malach. i. 2.)

MY GOD, I may tell You anything and everything. All I have to tell interests You, more especially the difficulties and troubles which do not easily come out to others, and are not for the most part very helpfully met when they do come out. "For what man knoweth the things of a man, but the spirit of a man that is in him?"[1]

But "the Spirit (of God) searcheth all things."[2] You know me through and through, and I am only owning to what You see and understand perfectly when I tell You of repinings aroused by gifts and opportunities bestowed on others, but denied to me. I find myself questioning, if not Your wisdom, at least Your love, in that I am less richly dowered than others with the happy temperament, the talents, the moral and social qualities that we reckon among the better gifts of life, that render life not a duty merely, nor a source of merit, but a continual joy. I do not see that "the lines are fallen unto me in goodly places;" rather I ask petulantly, "*Wherein hast Thou loved me?*"

The source of such disquiet is selfishness. This is the dismal consolation I should get were I to confide my trouble to the most indulgent of friends. But have You no better comfort for me, my Creator and my Father? To whom shall I go in my

---
[1] I Cor. ii.    [2] *Ibid.*

pains if not to Him Whose "hands have made me and formed me;"[1] to my Father "that hath possessed me, and made me, and created me;"[2] Who says to me, "I will have mercy on thee more than a mother?"[3] There is no humbling avowal I may not trust to You, and trusting it be sure of sympathy. "Why hast Thou done so to us?" was the meek remonstrance of the most submissive of handmaids. "Wherein hast Thou loved us?" was said by the most cross-grained and thankless of peoples. And to both questioners You vouchsafed a reply. I too, then, may ask: Why, Father, hast Thou done so to me? In withholding what is good in itself—what would have made me happier—*Wherein hast Thou loved me?*

Your answer might be: "Shall the thing formed say to Him that formed it, why hast Thou made me thus?"[4] But in place of rebuke You silence my trouble by an invitation: "Come up hither."[5] I am to take my stand by Your side, and from that height look around on the design framed from eternity. Parts of a plan can be viewed aright only in connection with the whole. To consider them independently is to miss not only the meaning and grandeur of the scheme in its entirety, but particular excellence also. This I know. Yet the tendency of selfishness is to contract the vision, and let the tiny portion assigned to itself in the universal design absorb the interest and warp the judgment. I am too near to earth, too involved in its passing interests to preserve the relative proportion necessary for viewing things aright. I must move further off—look forward a few years—plant my feet, not on this transitory world, but on the eternal shore, and from that standpoint look out upon creation.

"He hath begotten us...that we might be some beginning of His creature."[6]

---

1  Psa. cxviii.   2  Deut. xxxii.   3  Ecclus. iv.
4  Rom. ix.      5  Apoc. iv.      6  St. James i.

What an unsealing of eyes awaits me the moment after death! What a vista—all but infinite—will open out before me as the divine plan unfolds! All this human race, which, because it encloses my lot, is apt to engross my whole interest—if indeed my interest extends to the race and is not absorbed by the little miserable me—all this vast assemblage of human souls to be—but *some beginning of His creature!*

In eternity I shall see the part assigned to this beginning in the universal scheme. I shall see the part assigned to each unit. I shall grasp without effort, without reasoning, the self-evident fact that the dignity of every human being lies in its having a place in God's eternal design; that independent or solitary greatness is an impossibility; that our happiness no less than our grandeur consists in filling that place in the vast mosaic which divine wisdom and love has appointed us; that the significance of the creature, its beauty and well-being, are to be found only in its conformity with the ideal in the Creator's mind. Those who on earth have worked out that ideal and thereby reached their appointed place are happy. Those who, absorbed by selfish aims, have failed to fit themselves for the place assigned them, are necessarily cast aside as failures—and this whatever the gifts, station or influence that distinguished them in the momentary interval between two eternities that we call Time. Nothing indeed will astound me more than the reversal of lots in the world beyond the grave. I shall see how, in innumerable instances, paths of glory have led to everlasting confusion and oblivion. How, on the other hand, the unnoticed, the meagrely gifted, have made their way up to the highest honour, and are placed "with the princes of His people." The beggar of the Roman streets, shunned by every passerby, the shepherdess of an obscure village, the simple, illiterate Curé d'Ars, as "the friends of God are made exceedingly honourable." Whilst high above all, King of Kings and Lord of Lords, is a village Carpenter of heretofore.

Truly God's ways are not our ways! When I see as He sees, there will be no heartburnings, no pining for anything, however good in itself, that has not found place in His designs for me. Narrow views will melt away so completely as to be deemed wholly inexplicable in the past; egotism disappear in the burst of admiration at the design revealed in creation. What will be my delight to have a place—my particular place—in that glorious scheme! What my regret, as I turn away to purgatory, that I have failed to co-operate in the perfecting of the whole in the measure determined for me!

And this I shall see soon! Soon I shall be viewing all things from God's standpoint—the only one possible in the land of Truth. Recognising at last in my outfit a marvellous adaptation of means to the end, I shall see wherein He has loved me. I shall bless His will that has ordered all things sweetly. I shall trace His love in withholding as well as in giving, in ordaining my limitations and deficiencies no less than my aptitudes as means for attaining to my place in His kingdom. The greater or less glory and happiness of that place will be a matter of indifference to me. To reach the degree in which *He* would place me, to satisfy *Him*, to give Him throughout eternity the praise and reverence and service He asks of me—this will be the only ambition possible to my enlightened understanding and will. "In Thy light we shall see light."[1]

O Father, that it might be thus even now! That now, whilst my place in heaven is to be sought and reached, I might have the light and strength to accept, not with resignation only—this were too poor a gratitude—but with deepest, tenderest thankfulness, the means fashioned to my hand, designed by Your wisdom *for me!*

---

1 Psa. xxxv.

## XXXVIII

## *Twilight and Noon*

*My eyes are ever towards the Lord.*
(Psa. xxiv. 15.)

How marvellous is the vehemence of David's utterances when we consider the dimness with which God revealed Himself in the time of twilight before the coming of Christ! He was not altogether the hidden God. Throughout His dealings with His people we are struck by the mingling of light and darkness, distance and nearness, terrific chastisement and the tenderest blandishments of love. There was wonderful condescension and approach in the tabernacle of the wilderness, in the revelations to the prophets, in the interventions of mercy that times without number succoured the stiff-necked people. There are words of love in the Old Testament unsurpassed perhaps in tenderness by any in the New. Yet when His presence is nearest, when His reproaches are most touching, His words most endearing, we are conscious of the measureless difference between God's manifestation in the past and the intimacy and familiarity brought into our relations with Him by the Incarnation. We who live in the full illumination of that day which kings and prophets desired to see, cannot but feel how little earth's most enlightened men knew the God Who made them, before "the Word was made flesh and dwelt amongst us."

Yet so powerfully were they drawn to Him, that their words are the fittest exponents of every human heart when by desire, praise, affection or thanksgiving, it leaps up to God. They give expression to our every need. But, alas! they give too much matter also for self-reproach.

"*My eyes are always towards the Lord*," said David. God revealed Himself with special intimacy to the man according to His own Heart, that spoke in his own person of the sufferings and the glories of Him Who was to delight in the name of the Son of David. Yet, after all, what did David know of the Lord compared with the knowledge vouchsafed to the least enlightened of the Church's children! He had the memory of past mercies to the "seed of Abraham His servant, the sons of Jacob His chosen."[1] He had the shadowy presence of God in the Ark of the Covenant. And he had the dim foreknowledge of One to come, of the root of Jesse, "beautiful above the sons of men,"[2] yet "a worm, and no man, the reproach of men, and the outcast of the people,"[3] of "a Holy One Who should not see corruption,"[4] but "sit on the right hand of God till all His enemies be made His footstool."[5] This was all. But it was enough to keep the eyes of David fixed on God: "My eyes are always towards the Lord."

I think of myself. I think of the careful teaching from my childhood onwards: of the Gospel stories so familiar to me that I may follow the life of the God-man from His crib to His cross; living in His company; listening to His teaching; noting His look and gesture and act; studying His ways and dealings with men, His likes and dislikes, the human character which individualised Him and endeared Him to His friends. I may watch Him at His work, I may mark the effect upon Him of kindness and appreciation, and, on the other hand,

---

1  Psa. civ.            2  *Ibid.* xliv.        3  *Ibid.* xxi.
4  *Ibid.* xv.          5  *Ibid.* cix.

of ingratitude, scorn, cruelty and hate. I may see him thirsty, wayworn, footsore, and feast the eyes of my soul on the absolute perfection with which all the eventualities of life were met by Him Who, very God of very God, was yet the Son of Man and one of us.

Again, I may contemplate Him abiding ever with His Church, the source of every supernatural act throughout its length and breadth. I may see the Divine sap flowing through the vine to its furthest extremities, the principle of life and growth, of beauty and of fruitfulness in every soul His grace has sanctified. I know that all His merits are placed at my disposal; that He desires to make the meanest actions of my life meritorious of an eternal reward by uniting them with His. I have his invitation in the early morning to offer with Him His daily sacrifice that is offered for me. I hear Him asking of me, if not a daily, at least a frequent invitation to my heart. I hear him calling "Come aside and rest a little" when in afternoon hours the day's tasks are lightening; calling me to Him for an evening blessing when the day's work is done. Through the long hours of day and night His eye is following me—how often are my eyes towards the Lord?

O eager heart of David, that has met, if not with adequate response, at least with all your strength, the advances of our God, become to ours the stimulus they so sadly need! In our noontide splendour, in the fulness of fruition, we turn back to catch the glowing heat of your desires: "*O God my God, to Thee do I watch at break of day. For Thee my soul hath thirsted; for Thee my flesh, oh, how many ways!*"[1]

Your envying of our happier days and higher privileges shall make us appreciate them better: "They have seen Thy goings, O God, the goings of my God, of my King Who is in His sanctuary."[2]

---

1  Psa. lxii.   2  *Ibid.* lxvii.

We will prize His sanctuary in our midst; the sanctuary nearest to us, where most of all our homage and our love are due. Morning, afternoon, and evening we will seek Him there to bless Him and be blessed. "In the churches bless ye God the Lord."[1] "Seek ye the Lord, and be strengthened, seek His face evermore."[2]

---

[1] Psa. lxvii.   [2] *Ibid.* civ.

## XXXIV

## *Responsibility*

*Behold I and my children, whom God hath given me.*
(Heb. ii.)

No sympathy is so genuine and so ready, none so acceptable and helpful as that created by similarity of experience. "What doth he know that hath not been tried?"[1] "Who can rejoice with them that rejoice, and weep with them that weep"[2] like one whose heart has thrilled with the same gladness, and found relief in the same tears? Nothing more endears our Lord to us than the proofs of fellow-feeling that come out in every act of His human life. The Incarnation was the supreme gift of His sympathy. Every weary journey to and fro, every cure of soul or body, every word of warning and of comfort spoke of His sympathy. The Eucharist is His sympathy incarnate to the end of time.

No burden of ours is unshared by the Son of man. He has devised expedients that bewilder us by their condescension, in order to bring home to us the truth: "I also have a heart as well as you."[3] He will weep with his friends beside a grave. He will cower before pain and ignominy. He will be "tempted in all things like as we are."[4] Nay, He will even clothe Himself with the appearance of sin, be "made sin for us;"[5] feel its burden and its shame; bear the penalty of its guilt, to prove His devotedness

---

1 Ecclus. xxxiv.  2 Rom. xii.  3 Job xii.
4 Heb. iv.  5 2 Cor. v.

to us in His most winning of ways—the sharing of our miseries out of love.

All the heavy-laden He invites to Him, but none, perhaps, are more tenderly welcomed than those who come bowed beneath the weight of responsibility. Whether this devolves upon them through their relations with others as superiors, or is the consequence of kinship or friendship, it surely wins for them the sympathy of Him Who knows by His own experience the nature of all such responsibilities and the solicitude they entail.

"You call Me Master, and Lord, and you say well, for so I am."[1] "Is not He thy Father that hath possessed thee, and made thee and created thee?"[2] "As one whom the mother caresseth, so will I comfort you."[3] He is our Elder Brother, "first-born amongst many brethren;"[4] "the Physician of Whom we all have need;"[5] "the Shepherd and Bishop of our souls."[6] He knows, therefore, experimentally, the peculiar trials of the charge with which we are laden, and we may pour out our hearts to Him with the freedom that comes of perfect trust in One "sorrowful," "heavy," "troubled"—"in all things like as we are."[7]

My cares, dear Lord, are known to You, and not known only, but laid upon me by Your own hand. They weigh heavily at times. The interests at stake are so tremendous, and my ignorance and helplessness so great. Often enough I do not see what to do for the best; oftener still I cannot take the course that seems to me best. I am afraid of a false step; I am afraid of missing opportunities. Where to make a stand, and where to yield; when to command, and when to entreat; when to offer a word of remonstrance or of counsel, and when to say nothing and trust to prayer—all these are perplexities in which I need

---

1  John xiii.  
2  Deut. xxxii.  
3  Isa. lxvi.  
4  Rom. viii.  
5  Luke v.  
6  I Peter ii.  
7  Heb. iv.

and pray for the guidance of Your holy Spirit. There is a time to speak and a time to keep silence, but this is Your secret, O Lord! Give me the opportunities won by long prayer. Put upon my lips the well-timed word. Send me the success that comes of casting out the nets at Your word, under Your eye, with Your blessing.

And solve for me other problems—how to teach my children to take their place befittingly in the world without being of the world; how to train them for the battle of life; to provide them with an equipment for mind and heart that will suffice for the needs of these perilous times; to strengthen them by self-knowledge, self-reverence and self-control against the intellectual and moral dangers they will have to face, and prepare them for the burning questions of the day before they are flung into their midst. I tremble at the sight of these dangers beginning so early now when life is lived so fast. And the mother's words, the mother's arms do not reach as far as heretofore. She can only pray and trust. How earnestly You bid us trust, O Lord!

"Fear not: for the battle is not yours, but God's."[1] "Cast thy care upon the Lord, and He shall sustain thee."[2] "Be quiet, fear not, and let not thy heart be afraid."[3]

"I shall fear but I will trust in Thee."[4] "My God is my helper, and in Him will I put my trust."[5] "In my affliction I called upon the Lord, and I cried to my God."[6] "How long, O Lord, wilt Thou forget me, how long dost Thou turn away Thy face from me? Consider, and hear me, O Lord my God."[7]

"Behold I and my children, whom God hath given me!" I gather them round me here at Your feet. I trust them to Your care. Keep them in Your faith and in Your love, and bring

---

1  2 Par. xx.  2  Psa. liv.  3  Isa. vii.
4  Psa. lv.  5  Ibid. xvii.  6  Ibid.
7  Ibid. xii.

them safely through the dark perils of this life to the haven of salvation.

"*Behold I and my children, whom God hath given me.*" Let me say this one day as we stand in the brightness of Your Presence. Let me say in the fulness of my joy: "Of them whom Thou hast given me, I have not lost one."[1]

"Fear not! stand and see the great wonders of the Lord, which He will do."[2] "I will seek that which was lost, and that which was driven away, I will bring again; and I will bind up that which was broken, and I will strengthen that which was weak."[3] "I will give them life everlasting; and they shall not perish for ever, and no man shall pluck them out of My hand."[4]

---

1 John xvii.     2 Exod. xiv.     3 Ezech. xxxiv.
4 John x.

## XL

## *Life*

*As long as the heir is a child, he is under tutors and governors until the time appointed by the father.*
(Galat. iv. 1, 2.)

LIFE is a school—neither more nor less. *Not more.* Therefore we must not expect to find it satisfying. We must not look here for the freedom, the gladness, the warmth, the indefinable happiness of home.

But surely the eternal Home is worth waiting for! "It hath not yet appeared what we shall be."[1] "Eye hath not seen, nor ear heard, neither hath it entered into the heart of man, what things God hath prepared for them that love Him."[2] Yet we may infer something of the grandeur and blessedness of the life to come from the study of our own souls, from the vastness of their capacity, their insatiable thirst for knowledge, the depth and tenderness of their affections. Capacity supposes complement. The aspirations God has given He will surely satisfy. And therefore all that the noblest, the most highly gifted, the most loving of our race have desired for their perfect happiness, will be given to them in a fulness of which they can form no conception—"good measure, pressed down, shaken together, running over."[3] The most far-reaching penetration of the secrets of nature and of grace; the perfect realisation and more a thousand times than realisation of home; the satisfaction of

---

[1] John iii.  [2] I Cor ii.  [3] Luke vi.

all the cravings of kindred and of friendship, to say nothing of the essential joy of which these are but the redundance—this is what awaits us hereafter. Not here, nor yet. We must not look now for anything but the faintest anticipation of what is in store for us—*we are at school.*

How is it that this elementary truth has so little hold upon us? Life would be much less of a disappointment if we remembered its true character and purport; if we had more of the wisdom of the schoolboy who lives with his heart in the future, and for the rough discipline of the present is for ever promising himself the compensations of home.

Life is a school. *Nothing less.* Therefore we must beware of squandering the time given us to prepare for our final state. We are here for our training, not for our enjoyment, and must go in for the experiences and the work our education demands. We have to drill ourselves in regard to our pleasures and our pains. Pleasure must not be suffered to monopolize our interest. It is but the half holiday thrown into school life to make its pressure bearable. Pain must not cast us down utterly, but detach us from our surroundings here; and foster in us the homesickness of the saints. And we have to work—work seriously at the formation of mind and heart—the task allotted us in this world. Both have to be conformed to the likeness of Him Who is the pattern of all the elect. Both have to be brought into harmony with the surroundings in which they will find themselves directly. "Let this mind be in you, which was also in Christ Jesus."[1] "Our conversation must be in heaven."[2]

Meantime we have with us—not only as Master, but as Father and Elder Brother—Him Who has passed through the experience of human life; Who, "because the children are partakers of flesh and blood, hath also Himself in like manner

---
1   Philip ii.          2   *Cf. Ibid.* iii.

been partaker of the same,"[1] "like to us in all things excepting sin;"[2] Whose word of comfort, as we take to Him our weary tasks, is a reminder at once of their necessity and of their recompense: "Work your work before the time, and He will give you your reward in His time."[3]

My God, I thank You for the immortal spirit You have given me. I thank You for its vast capacity, which I recognise in a craving that nothing here can sate. Its very neediness appeals to Your beneficence: "abyss calleth upon abyss."[4] Keep up the keenness of its desire, the hunger and thirst which You have declared blessed, till the time comes for satisfying it fully. Let me not seek to assuage it by anything transitory. Let me "so pass through the things of time as not to forfeit those of eternity."[5] Let me be schooled by the tasks and trials, the little joys and sorrows and passing brightnesses of this life for the great future—the true life that lies beyond. May my happiness, no less than my duty, be found in preparing now for what I am to do and to be hereafter.

And when my school days are over and my lessons here are learned—dear Father, take me Home!

---

1  Heb. ii.   2  *Ibid.* iv.   3  Ecclus. li.
4  Psa. xii.   5  Collect for 3rd Sunday after Pentecost.

Additional titles available from
# St. Augustine Academy Press
Books for the Traditional Catholic

### Titles by Mother Mary Loyola:
Blessed are they that Mourn
Confession and Communion
Coram Sanctissimo (Before the Most Holy)
First Communion
First Confession
Forgive us our Trespasses
Hail! Full of Grace
Heavenwards
Holy Mass/How to Help the Sick and Dying
Home for Good
Jesus of Nazareth: The Story of His Life Written for Children
The Child of God: What comes of our Baptism
The Children's Charter
The Little Children's Prayer Book
The Soldier of Christ: Talks before Confirmation
Welcome! Holy Communion Before and After

### Titles by Father Lasance:
The Catholic Girl's Guide
The Young Man's Guide

### Tales of the Saints:
A Child's Book of Saints by William Canton
A Child's Book of Warriors by William Canton
Illustrated Life of the Blessed Virgin by Rev. B. Rohner, O.S.B.
Legends & Stories of Italy by Amy Steedman
Mary, Help of Christians by Rev. Bonaventure Hammer
The Book of Saints and Heroes by Lenora Lang
Saint Patrick: Apostle of Ireland
The Story of St. Elizabeth of Hungary by William Canton

Check our Website for more:
## www.staugustineacademypress.com

www.ingramcontent.com/pod-product-compliance
Lightning Source LLC
Chambersburg PA
CBHW032010040426
42448CB00006B/565